"It is good to see a discussion open about one of the precious gifts God has given us. I appreciate that Pastor Wong has tackled this subject with a deep desire to draw from the Scriptures a theology of sex. Prepare for an honest and insightful discussion."
—Dr. Darryl DelHousaye, President of Phoenix Seminary

"In our postmodern society, personal opinion and whatever feels right to the individual reigns. And this has permeated the way we think about everything, including person-hood, marriage, and sexual morality. Corwin provides a biblical and simple pattern by which the church might come to a biblical worldview concerning God's design for people in marriage and sexual morality. This topic is too important to not address, and Corwin's handling of it makes it accessible and implementable for all willing to engage the topic."
—Paul Abeyta (Pastor)

"Corwin Wong has written a book we all need to read. There is a tremendous need to call Christians back to sexual purity and what that actually means. You may not agree with everything he says, but you will be challenged to think outside of your own box. This book will speak to your head and your heart. I am happy to recommend it to you!"
—Rev Greg Speck, Youth and Family Communicator, author of *Sex, It's Worth Waiting For, Living for Jesus Beyond the Spiritual High, Build to Last,* and *Mustard Seeds on Youth Ministry*

"Corwin Wong has written a much needed book for pastors and laymen alike, looking faithfully and helpfully at the wonderful, sometimes confusing, and often difficult gift of sex. Wong writes on the topic with openness, wisdom, and theological acumen. It is a book that was waiting to be written and one that should be on every pastor's shelf."
—*Dr. John Shouse*

PLUM
A THEOLOGY OF SEX

A Guide To
Honoring God
With Your Body

Corwin Wong

RIVER BIRCH PRESS

Mobile, Alabama

Contents

To Christ, the local church, and my wife,
all whom I love and who have loved me greatly

Acknowledgments

Thank you to all those who were open to having candid conversations with me about many sensitive areas when it comes to sexuality and marriage; every conversation mattered. Especially to my wife, Mandy, who was a direct contributor to this Bible study as God convicted us and sanctified us through His Word and blessed our marriage greatly because of it. She trusted me in implementing principles of P.L.U.M. in our marriage, and I am thankful for how God has grown me as a husband and father because of it.

Preface

"Just pray about it, and whatever you and your spouse agree upon is the right answer for you."

This is the summary of most of the advice I would hear from other Christians, pastors, and mentors concerning many of the more difficult questions when it comes to sex in marriage. It is also descriptive of the advice that I would read in many Christian marriage/sex books. The gist of this advice, is that if a husband and wife prayerfully agree on something, they can be confident that they are moving forward in God's will for the sake of unity in their marriage. The notion of two spouses simply coming to an agreement on something through prayer sets a troubling precedent that has been used as a principle for many areas in Christian living.

Mandy and I experienced a lot of dissatisfaction during our first year (and most difficult year) of marriage as we came to understand that there was a variety of advice coming from Christian sources to difficult questions concerning sex in marriage that had little to no biblical support. This dissatisfaction resulted in one of the biggest blessings to our marriage, and this book explains our journey through the Bible as it pertains to sexual purity in all areas of life. The theological foundation presented in this book has implications for those who are single, dating, young, old, married, divorced, remarried, widowed, abused, sexually confused, post-menopausal, and more.

Discovering and knowing God's will for Christian living is nothing mysterious in which the answers will be found through new and/or special revelation. Everything that pertains to Christian living can be found in the infallibility of the Word of God, the Bible. It may not always be easy to come to an agreement on all matters concerning Christian morality, but Christians have the responsibility to search diligently through the Scriptures and to allow God's Word to be the guide for even the most difficult and controversial conversations.

There is more than enough grace for genuine believers to come to different convictions on secondary (non-salvation related) matters, but that does not excuse the responsibility for each person to continually search the Scriptures while keeping in mind that their previous convictions may change through their deepening studies.

My hope and prayer is that the theological foundation presented in this book will help you think more critically and biblically concerning sexual purity. You might even disagree with some of the views presented in this book, but I just hope that your disagreement is based upon strong biblical evidence, and not just your own opinions. The overall goal of this book is to provide P.L.U.M. as a consistent theological framework that guides the Christian towards protecting the sanctity of sex in all situations.

1
Sex and Worship

You were created in the image of God and so was your sexuality.

God created man in His own image, in the image of God he created him; male and female He created them (Genesis 1:27).

Humans are unique creations of God in the foundational sense that only we are created in His image. God gave us emotions, an eternal spirit, knowledge, and meaning in life. As God is all-controlling, He gave humans some sense of control in their own lives. As God is all-knowing, He gave humans the capacity to know Him and to understand that there is a Creator. As God created humans both male and female in His image, we can know that we can have a fuller understanding of the image of God through human sexuality. Therefore, if men and women are created in the image of God, and God created them to eventually come together in sexual union (Genesis 2:24), then human sexuality itself was created in the image of God.

If human sexuality is an expression of God's image, then the question is: What can we learn about God based on sexuality? The reason why answering this question is so important is because its answer should also help Christians answer other questions such as:

- How can a Christian couple decide when to start/stop trying to have children?

1

- How can Christians make informed decisions about birth control? Artificial insemination? Surrogacy? In vitro fertilization? Abortion? Cloning? Genetically modified human embryos? Adoption?
- What physical displays of affection are sinful between an unmarried man and woman? (How far is too far?)
- What is an appropriate frequency of sex in marriage?
- How is God's image still expressed in the sexuality of singleness?
- How can we know what is sexually sinful if it's not explicitly mentioned in the Bible? (oral sex, anal sex, fetishes, etc.)
- Is it okay for men to use sexual performance-enhancing drugs?
- How young is too young to get married and/or have children?

Do you have any questions about sex that you have not been able to find an answer for in the Bible? My prayer for you is that after learning about God's image from a human sexuality standpoint, you will have a biblical foundation leading you to a conviction that will equip you to honor God in all that you do and say. This book and the theological foundation it presents for sexual purity can be summed up by this statement:

> God created sex first to be an act of worship
> and secondly, a gift for men and women to enjoy.

When Christians understand this to be true, they will have a greater appreciation for the limits and restrictions God has placed on the expression of human sexuality. They will also remember how God's holy and perfect nature is so easily profaned by the sinful nature of men and women.

When we fall far short of God's holiness, it should remind us of our need for a Savior, the Lord Jesus Christ, and what His substitutionary atoning death accomplished for us who believe in Him for salvation—our ultimate restoration to holiness.

Three Things To Know Before Reading About God's Design for Sex

1. If you are a follower of Jesus Christ, then your body does not belong to you.

A common saying in our earthly, sinful world is, "It's my body, and I'll do what I want." This cannot be in the vocabulary of the Christian. Christians must remember that Jesus Christ paid the penalty on the cross by dying for their sins. Sin is simply doing what one chooses and not what God desires. The following verses are just a few examples of what I am talking about:

Or do you not know that your body is a temple of the Holy Spirit who is in you, whom you have from God, and that you are not your own? For you have been bought with a price: therefore, glorify God in your body (1 Corinthians 6:19-20 NASB).

For by Him (Jesus Christ) *all things were created, both in the heavens and on earth, visible and invisible, whether on thrones or dominions or rulers or authorities—all things have been created through Him and for Him* (Colossians 1:16).

For from Him and through Him and to Him are all things. To Him be the glory forever, Amen (Romans 11:36).

Understanding that our body is no longer our own when we place our faith in Jesus Christ for the forgiveness of our sins, the difficult task then becomes to renew our mind so that we can know the will of God. All of a sudden there is a shift from our life being a *right* to now becoming a *responsibility* to glorify God with. For those who do not follow Jesus, it doesn't matter what they do with their lives from an eternal perspective. Whether they live a life doing good deeds or not, they are without forgiveness for their sinful state and will not inherit eternal life regardless. In John 15 when Jesus talks about being the vine and His disciples being the branches, He meant that apart from faith in Him, we cannot do anything that pleases God. As long as a person is not resting on Jesus for their salvation, their sin is still separating them from God. They have no peace with God and are in need of reconciliation, which can only be accomplished through faith in Jesus Christ.

In this book about God's design for sex, it is not a self-help book about how to have better sex, prepare you for marriage, or the advantages of sexual purity. It is all about how the Christian is to honor God with their body and how to be conformed more to the likeness of Christ. As a consequence, those who focus on honoring God with their sexuality will experience more joy in their marital intimacy and have a greater appreciation for sexual purity. I cannot stress this enough: if you are a Christian, your sexuality is not a right, but it is a responsibility.

2. New sin revealed in your life does not mean you lost your salvation.

This book presents a theological foundation on how to discern what is sexually sinful. As we look at the four purposes of sex and how God designed them to be expressions of His image, there will be areas in your own sexual life (whether married or single) that will be brought up. I encourage you to hold it up to the lens of P.L.U.M. to see how that area might not be completely adhering to God's design for sex.

When those who are following Jesus Christ come under a new conviction of sin in their life, they feel as if they need to accept Jesus Christ as their Lord and Savior all over again in order to secure their salvation. This shouldn't be a surprise, after all, many preachers and pastors tend to preach in a way that leaves people feeling so guilty about their sin that those people may feel like they were never truly saved in the first place. Although I don't doubt that there are many people out there who profess to be followers of Christ but do not bear any Christian fruit of their profession. A true follower of Jesus Christ does not need to worry that as they grow in their knowledge of God's Word, sin will be revealed in their life.

Therefore there is now no condemnation for those who are in Christ Jesus (Romans 8:1).

In this passage of Romans, the Apostle Paul ends chapter 7 of his letter by sharing his own personal struggle with the never-ending battle of sin in his life, and how on one hand, he is seeking to please the LORD with his life, but yet on the other hand, he keeps finding himself doing the opposite.

Thanks be to God through Jesus Christ our Lord! So then, on the one hand I myself with my mind am serving the law of God, but on the other, with my flesh the law of sin (Romans 7:25).

Do you see the wonderful truth in these passages? The defining trait of a fruit-bearing Christian is not living a perfect life that is totally absent of all sin, rather it is upon discovering sin in their life, to have an attitude of remorse and repentance about it and a genuine desire to change the behavior. The conviction of sin should not scare a follower of Jesus, but it should affirm that they care about the things God cares about. When someone places their faith in Jesus Christ for the forgiveness of their sin, they are immediately forgiven of ALL their sin—past, present, and future.

3. ALL sin is worthy of death, and therefore all sin should be taken very seriously.

It is human nature to want to rank different kinds of sin or immoral activity by those that are very serious to those that are not so serious. After all, our justice system is set up in such a way where crimes have differing punishments, depending upon their severity, and rightfully so. Although this is an effective way of dealing with crime in a worldly society, it does not reflect how the kingdom of heaven works. God's standard for those who enter His kingdom is complete flawlessness.

Therefore you are to be perfect, just as your heavenly Father is perfect (Matthew 5:48).

Jesus clearly gives us God's perfect standard and expectation of God's children in this verse. In the context of the passage, Jesus is teaching how God's children need to love their enemies and how counter-cultural God's love is.

For whoever keeps the whole law and yet stumbles in one point, he has become guilty of all (James 2:10).

James was writing to a church that had been guilty of showing partiality towards the wealthy individuals in their fellowship while neglecting the poorer ones. He points out how the sin of partiality is just as serious as any other sin. In the church today, we often see many examples of how we have been conditioned to consider certain sins more severe than others. The sins that we don't consider to be very serious are deserving of the same consequence as the most serious of sins.

For all have sinned and fall short of the glory of God. Being justified as a gift by His grace through the redemption which is in Christ Jesus; whom God displayed publicly as a propitiation in His blood through faith. This was to demonstrate His righteousness, because in the forbearance of God He passed over the sins previously committed; for the demonstration I say, of His righteousness at the present time, so that He would be just and the justifier of the one who has faith in Jesus. Where then is boasting? It is excluded. By what kind of law? Of works? No, but by a law of faith (Romans 3:23-28).

In this passage, we can see that we will not come to perfection through our own efforts, but only through the work of Jesus Christ as being the only One who can justify us before God. In learning about God's design for sex, you will be challenged in your presuppositions in how you view all the various types of sexual expression. I hope learning about God's purposes for sex will strengthen your convictions as well as give you a clearer idea of what is sexually moral.

Do not judge so that you will not be judged. For in the way you judge, you will be judged; and by your standard of measure, it will be measured to you. Why do you look at the speck that is in your brother's eye, but do not notice the log that is in your own eye? Or how can you say to your brother, "Let me take that speck out of your eye" and behold, there is a log in your own eye? You hypocrite, first take the log out of your own eye, and then you will see clearly to take the speck out of your brother's eye (Matthew 7:1-5).

These words of Jesus are probably the most quoted by non-Christians than any other verses in the Bible. Unfortunately, they are likely taken out of context and misused from the way Jesus originally said them. Jesus is commanding His followers not to be critical of other's sin in a way that is condemning them. For those of us who truly want to help others with the sin in their life, we must first be aware of the sin in our own lives where we need the help of others. In being aware of our own sin, it will change how we approach others in their sin. Self-awareness will cause an individual to be more gracious and understanding towards others, all the while speaking truth in love to one another.

The most common thing to do when talking about sexual sin is to want to point out all the sexual sin in other people's lives. I challenge you to first look into your own life and see what implications God's purposes for sex has upon you. If you are someone who feels the need to correct others in their sin, you need to ask yourself, "Am I taking my own sin just as seriously?"

2

The Myth of Sexual Purity

How did you learn about sex?

As for me, I learned about sex in the way most young men learn about sex—from my friends. I was first introduced to what sexual intercourse is in fifth grade when I happened to see a cartoon book at my friend's house that was titled, "Mommy, where did I come from?" I couldn't help but pick up the book; and to my surprise, for the first time I saw drawings of people having sex, let alone naked people. Strangely enough, I didn't think much about sex after seeing that book. It wasn't until a couple years later when I was hanging out at another friend's house after school. This friend of mine collected comic cards with his dad. It was a huge hobby of theirs that included going to comic book conventions almost every month.

One day when we and a couple more friends were the only ones at his house after school, my friend decided to show us the "forbidden" card collections. These forbidden cards were kept in huge binders inside a large china hutch with glass doors. Before that day, we had never bothered to even ask what were in the binders, because we just assumed they were really rare, really expensive comic book characters that his dad was really protective of. You can imagine the anticipation and excitement we all had when my friend decided to open the china hutch doors to the forbidden cards.

A moment later my teenage world was changed forever. As my friend laid the closed binder down on the floor and the four of us boys gathered anxiously around the binder as if we had just discovered lost treasure, he opened it. The binder was certainly filled with cards, but they weren't comic cards. They were all cards of fully naked women on them. As a boy who was raised in a Christian home, I knew what I was looking at was wrong. Even though I had never had any kind of conversation about sex with my parents, I somehow knew that what I was looking at was sinful.

Unfortunately I was only intrigued to see more of what I had seen at my friend's house, leading me to look at pornography with my friends anytime we had sleepovers at each other's houses. It ultimately led to a fascination, and at times an addiction, to pornography. Little did I know that all the pornographic images I was taking into my brain would damage and negatively change my view of sexuality for the rest of my life.

As I was involved in my youth group at church and went to many church winter and summer camps, I learned a lot about the Christian view of sex. The only thing I got out of it was: Don't have sex until you're married. So I didn't. By God's grace alone, I was able to remain a virgin until I married my wife.

So you can imagine how I was feeling on my wedding day. Here I was, about to marry the most beautiful woman in the world, and I was only hours away from the wedding night! Just a few hours later the wedding was over and we got to our hotel, and that night was AWFUL! I don't know about other married men, but I didn't expect there to be so much laughing during sex. When we first saw each other naked, we laughed. When we "tried" having sex, we laughed even more! We never actually completed the consummation of our marriage that night. I thought to myself, *It's okay, you have the entire honeymoon to enjoy it!*

There wasn't much more laughing during the honeymoon.

In fact there wasn't much sex during the honeymoon either. I probably had similar expectations that most guys have for their honeymoons, and that is "All sex, all the time!" Our honeymoon was filled with arguments and awkward silences, all centered on the topic of sex. To help ease the tension, we bought a few jigsaw puzzles from a local store and spent much of our time putting those together (our honeymoon was in South Lake Tahoe in the middle of May).

We were so desperate to try to have a good time on our honeymoon, we even invited our newlywed friends to join us the last couple days. They even stayed in the other room of our hotel suite! Unfortunately, I learned during the first year of marriage that even though I was technically a virgin, I was anything but sexually pure.

My wife, Mandy, and I received several Christian marriage books during our first year of marriage to help guarantee that we would have a godly and blessed marriage. Sure enough, there was at least one chapter in each of those books that focused on sex, and a couple of the books were entirely about sex. I will never forget how, while we were dating, Mandy had so much respect for me as a man for the fact that I saved myself sexually for marriage. However, it became clear on our wedding night and the week of our honeymoon that Mandy and I had very different expectations of what sex was supposed to be like in a God-loving marriage.

What I hadn't realized before the wedding night was just how deceived I was into thinking that I was sexually pure. I believe I expected the same things that most husbands would expect from their wives on their wedding night and honeymoon: 1) I expected to have a lot of sex (like, every waking moment that we weren't eating or sleeping); 2) I expected my wife to wear really sexy things; 3) I expected my wife to be just as excited about having sex as I was. As it turned out, my expectations were way off.

The reason why I had these expectations was because of what I grew up learning about sex through the American culture and media. I realized that virginity alone did not make me sexually pure in God's eyes because I was sexually impure in my heart and mind. My struggle with pornography during middle school and high school, along with all the movies and television shows that I had seen that promoted sexual sin, had given me a severely distorted view on what godly marital sex should look like. I failed to do what I mentioned in the first chapter: I failed to consider all my sins seriously. I downplayed the fact that to even look lustfully at a woman was just as serious in God's eyes as actually committing the physical act of adultery (Matthew 5:27-28).

A dangerous view of sexual purity that is common in the American church is what I call "sexual moralism." Like all other forms of moralism, its theme is that people can be good based on whether they do what is right and abstain from doing what is wrong. This is a common form of heresy in the Christian faith. Many times Christians are guilty of promoting moralism in that they judge their faith based on how "good" they are. This is the same form of self-righteous based faith that the Pharisees were accused of by Jesus.

The idea that a young Christian can remain sexually pure is simply impossible because "all have sinned and fall short of the glory of God" (Romans 3:23). If you take the reality of our utter sinfulness and depravity before God, you can know that you NEVER had a chance of being pure by any means! We are all impure before God and in need of atonement for our sins through faith in Christ alone and His atoning sacrifice in His death and resurrection.

Unfortunately, Christians tend to use mere scare tactics when giving younger Christians wisdom on sexual purity, like:

- "If you have sex before marriage, it will ruin your future relationship with your spouse."
- "If you get pregnant as a teenager, it will ruin your life."
- "If you have sex with multiple people, you'll get a disease."

Although these statements are potentially true, these should not be the basis of our obedience to God and His commandments. The foundational purpose for living an obedient lifestyle to the Lord should be solely out of one's love for Him—nothing more, nothing less. Jesus summed up all the commandments and stated that loving God and loving your neighbor as yourself are the two greatest commandments (Matthew 22:36-40).

In R.A. Torrey's book, *The Person and Work of the Holy Spirit*, Torrey put it this way:

> How often some young man has had his hand on the door of some place of sin that he is about to enter and the thought has come to him, "If I should enter there, my mother may hear of it and it would nearly kill her," and he has turned his back on that door and gone away to lead a pure life, that he might not grieve his mother. But there is One who I holier than any mother, One who is more sensitive against sin than the purest woman who ever walked this earth, and who loves us as even no mother ever loved. This One dwells in our hearts, if we are really Christians, and He sees every act we do by day or under cover by night; He hears every word we utter in public or private; He sees every thought we entertain, He beholds every fancy and imagination that is permitted even a momentary lodging in our mind, and if there is anything unholy, impure, selfish, mean, petty, unkind, harsh, unjust, or any evil act or word or thought or fancy, He is grieved by it.

The Christian's motivation to abstain from sexual sin cannot be the false notion that somehow they can be sexually pure because they cannot. The motivation for the Christian to abstain from sexual sin needs to be purely out of their love for God and their desire to not want to do anything that grieves Him, knowing how much He hates sin and the great lengths He went to redeem us from that which He hates so much.

Imagine a teenage girl who has been told that if she were to get pregnant in her teenage years, it would ruin her life; and behold, she became pregnant! How do you think she would feel about her future at that point? She would likely feel hopeless in many ways. She might consider abortion to try to right her wrongs because she doesn't consider herself worthy of being a mother simply due to her early pregnancy.

The problem with using fear tactics in teaching about abstaining from sin is that it does not communicate the redemptive aspect of the Gospel. God redeems all things in our lives for His glory. Since Christians will continue to sin in their earthly lives, it is harmful and incorrect to think that somehow their lives can be ruined in a way that thwarts God's sovereignty in completing the work He began in them.

Sexual sin does not always result in guilt, pain, and regret as the fear tactics would have people believe. Many people are completely content and satisfied with indulging in all their sexual desires, thus rejecting God's offer of forgiveness for their sins.

Those who have committed sins in their lives that have resulted in greater consequences than other sins need to know that their hope should not be placed in their ability to live perfect lives, rather in the fact that regardless of when they sin again, God's grace is even greater (Romans 5).

Sex Can Be Used Sinfully in Marriage

The arguments and disappointments around sex dominated the first year of our marriage, and we were scrambling for answers on how to deal with it. The lustful issues that I struggled with through my teenage and young adult years affected the way I went about sex in my marriage. I found myself putting ungodly expectations upon my wife that were also at many times, unloving. I found myself doing almost anything for her to have sex with me, even if it meant getting her to feel guilty for not doing it. Once when I was praying about our marriage, it occurred immediately after one of our more heated arguments surrounding our sex life. I eventually was brought to my knees in prayer on the living room floor of our first apartment while Mandy was still in the bedroom trying to gather her thoughts as well. All of a sudden Philippians 2:3 popped in my mind: "Do nothing out of selfish ambition or vain conceit, but with humility of mind, consider others better than yourselves." I was immediately convicted of the fact that I had a completely selfish perspective of what sex should be in a marriage. Throughout this book, the operating definition of "selfish" is as follows: to desire one's own will over God's will.

Moments after that conviction, I felt as if God were asking me, "Corwin, if I were to completely remove sex from your marriage, would you love Mandy the way that I command a husband to love his wife (like in Ephesians 5)?" Sadly, the honest answer to that question at the time was no. That is when I realized that even in marriage, sex can be used sinfully and selfishly. I know so many other Christian husbands who, like me, viewed sex in marriage as if it were some kind of duty that their wives had to fulfill whenever the husband felt he needed it.

After spending our whole first year of marriage trying to place the blame on Mandy, saying things to myself like, "Things would be great if we just had more sex," or "She's not meeting my needs, and it's causing me to struggle sexually," God humbled me by making me realize that there was sin in my life that I had to deal with. And this is what led me to the Bible study that I am sharing with you. I set out to understand what God has to say about sex in His Word. I wanted to better understand God's purposes for sex.

I know husbands who demand that their wives have sex with them no less frequently than every three days. One time I was talking to a Christian brother of mine who was engaged at the time, and he went on to explain to me that he expects to have sex at least five days a week, and to him, that was a very modest number! Mandy and I would often read in those Christian marriage/sex books about how important it is for the husband to communicate their sexual needs to their wives. At first it seemed like a brilliant idea! Why shouldn't I tell my wife when I am feeling the need for sexual intimacy? After all, I'm sure the last thing my wife wants is for me to seek the solutions to my sexual needs elsewhere, right?

After coming to the conclusion through Scripture that my view of marital sex was completely and utterly selfish and sinful, I came to also realize how wrong it is for me to claim that I have some kind of required quota of sex that needs to be fulfilled in order for me to be the most loving husband I can possibly be. It is as if I, as well as just about every other man on earth, was brought up to learn that sex is something that men need, or they will die!

When Jesus gave the difficult teaching about how divorce was never something that God approved of, and that no one should separate what God has joined together, the disciples began to question whether or not it was worth getting married at all! Then Jesus said in Matthew 19:11-12:

Not all men can accept this statement, but only those to whom it has been given. For there are eunuchs who were born that way from their mother's womb; and there are eunuchs who were made eunuchs by men; and there are also eunuchs who made themselves eunuchs for the sake of the kingdom of heaven. He who is able to accept this, let him accept it.

Do you hear what Jesus is saying? Not all men are called to marry. That means that a man who does not have sex is still fully equipped by God to live a life glorifying to Him. The fact of whether or not a man has sex should not be a factor of whether or not they are able to be the kind of person that God requires him to be. This means that husbands cannot use the excuse of, "Well, honey, maybe if we had sex more often then I wouldn't be struggling so much with pornography." or "Honey, I feel that if we just had sex more often then I wouldn't be so grumpy, and I would be more willing to help around the house." The Apostle Paul says strikingly similar things when it comes to single and married men in 1 Corinthians 7:32-35:

But I want you to be free from concern. One who is unmarried is concerned about the things of the Lord, how he may please the Lord; but one who is married is concerned about the things of the world, how he may please his wife, and his interests are divided. The woman who is unmarried, and the virgin, is concerned about things of the Lord, that she may be holy in body and spirit; but one who is married is concerned about the things of the world, how she may please her husband. This I say for your own benefit; not to put a restraint upon you, but to promote what is appropriate and to secure undistracted devotion to the Lord.

Key phrases in this passage are: "how he may please the Lord" and "undistracted devotion to the Lord." This passage makes it clear that the desire for sexual intimacy should not be a factor in a believer's ability to be devoted to the Lord as He commands them to.

Sexual purity in marriage is often dwindled down to not committing adultery, whether physically or of the heart. However, it should be seen that sex can be used impurely in the context of marriage in many other ways other than men looking at pornography and spouses committing adultery against one another.

3

Loopholes of Christian Sex Education

Through this process of conviction that I was dealing with concerning my sexual sin, it became apparent to me just how much my Christian sex education had failed me. I had heard about so many things that were considered sinful, and all the benefits of why it was so important to abstain until marriage (more Christian moralism). However, I never truly learned the "why" reasons for sexual sin. There are many good reasons, even for the unbeliever, to practice safe and healthy sex. However, in a world where technological advances are coupled with the ever-changing morals of society, the main question that jumps to my mind when wanting to know what is sexually sinful is why?

What I also noticed in Christian sex education is that often-times it seemed to avoid many of the most difficult questions, such as:

- Why is homosexual marriage considered sinful if the two people are lovingly devoted to each other in the same way a husband and wife should be?
- When is it too young to marry?
- Why is it sinful for a boyfriend and girlfriend to live to-gether even though they are more committed than some married couples?
- How far is too far before marriage, and why?
- Is it okay for Christian married couples to not want kids?

- When should married couples start having kids?
- Is masturbation always considered sinful?
- What does the Bible say about artificial insemination or fertilization?
- Does the Bible support the use of artificial birth control?

One of the things that bothered me the most about the Christian marriage books I read, were they all seemed to be saying the same thing to husbands in regards to how to get their wives to have sex more often. To paraphrase them, that advice would often be, "Husbands, if you do lots of nice and selfless acts, your wives will want to have sex with you." But what happens when that husband starts doing those nice and selfless acts (cleaning the house, doing the dishes, giving his wife foot massages, taking on more responsibilities concerning the children), and his wife does not react the way that the Christian marriage books say she will?

Two things will likely happen as a result: 1) the husband will start thinking that his wife is the problem in the marriage, 2) the husband will become embittered in his acts of kindness and may or may not continue in doing them. The problem is that the husband was not doing acts of kindness out of the kind of love that Christ had for the Church when He gave Himself up for her. Instead, the husband was doing acts of kindness out of an attitude of selfishness, motivated by the anticipation of a certain reaction from his wife.

Romans 5:8 speaks of the love of Christ in that He died to save people while they were still sinners. This means that God was patient with me for the first 15 years of my life before I placed my faith in His Son, Jesus Christ. While I was still a condemned sinner, God's provision was made available to me the entire time even though I wanted nothing to do with Him.

For the husband hoping to have more sex with his wife, sex should not be his motivation to do acts of kindness for his wife; his love for God and desire to be obedient to Him should be his main motivation. The real test is whether or not the husband is willing to give himself up for his wife regardless of whether or not it will result in her wanting to have sex.

What I feel is missing from Christian sex education is a theological foundation on which the Christian can make their decisions and convictions concerning sexuality. It seems that the church as a whole tends to give very practical advice to Christians, but their theological foundation falls apart if the situation becomes more complicated. In reality, good and proper theology will give consistent guidance regardless of how complicated the situation is.

My hope is that through understanding God's purposes for sex through P.L.U.M., every Christian will know the deeper answers to the "why" questions when it comes to sexual morality. The answer "because the Bible says so" does not do justice to God's beautiful design for sex and to the practicality and implications of how we are all created in His wonderful image.

Sex is first an act of worship, and secondly, a gift for men and women to enjoy

God created man and woman in His image, therefore, we are created to reflect His image in all that we say and do. Just as all of creation was designed to reflect His majesty (Romans 1:20), men and women were created in His image for the sole purpose of glorifying Him (Genesis 1:27, 1 Corinthians 6:19-20). Far too often, the Christian view of sex tends to focus far too heavily on the presupposition that God created sex as a gift for husbands and wives to enjoy.

21

Instead, I would like to see all Christians understand this about sex: God first created sex to be an act of worship, and secondly as a gift for men and women to enjoy—all for His glory. In other words, if Christians keep in mind that their sexuality is to be an act of worship, it will help them remember that there are proper and improper ways of expressing that sexuality. If Christians focus too heavily on the gift aspect of sex, then they will likely be able to justify virtually any sexual conduct that they find pleasure in, so as long as it is mutual and seems good to them.

In the next several chapters, I will take you through the five-step journey I set out on when discovering the purposes of sex, what they meant, and the conclusion I came to afterward.

Step 1: Establish the purpose for living

What is the chief end of man? To glorify God and enjoy Him forever. 1 Corinthians 10:31, Colossians 1:16 (Westminster Catechism).

The very foundation of Christian living is summed up by Jesus in Mark12:29-31:

> *The foremost (command) is, "Hear, Or Israel! The Lord our God is one Lord, and you shall love the Lord your God with all your heart, and with all your soul, and with all your mind, and with all your strength." The second is this, "You shall love your neighbor as yourself." There is no other commandment greater than these.*

By starting my journey with this foundation in mind, it served as a constant reminder that whatever I was to discover about God's purposes for sex, the answer I would be looking for would lead me to be concerned with glorifying God first and foremost, regardless of the implication it might have on my life.

Step 2: Establish the purposes of sex in the Bible

After one has settled with this understanding in regards to the purpose of life on earth, then the second step is to understand that if men and women were created in God's image (which means their sexuality was also created in His image), how does sexuality reflect His image? To answer this question, we must look throughout the entirety of the Bible to find how sex was used throughout Biblical history. All of the Bible's teachings on sex and sexual sin can be narrowed down to four distinct purposes for sex: Pleasure, love, unity, and multiplying (P.L.U.M.).

Step 3: Find the significance of each purpose

The third step of discovering God's purposes for sex is to answer this question: if these (P.L.U.M.) are the four purposes of sex, then how do they each reflect God's image?

After this question is answered, that is when the Christian can move on to step four: putting it all together and consider the implications of what it looks like to properly reflect God's image through sexuality.

Step 4: Find the commonality of all sexual sin

Step 5: Conclusion

Reflection Questions:

- What kinds of questions do you hope to have answered from this book?
- How well do you think the church has done in teaching about sexual morality and its various topics?

- What topics would you want to hear more about in your church concerning sexual morality?
- If you're married, what was your sexual relationship like at the beginning of your marriage? How has it changed? In what ways did the Bible guide you in this area?
- If you're single, what do you anticipate the sexual relationship to be like in marriage? From where do you think you get these ideas?

4

More Pleasurable Than Sex

Pleasure—the P in P.L.U.M.. (The four purposes do not need to be in any particular order, it's just that P.L.U.M. seems to be the better alternative than MULP, LUMP, or ULMP!)

When my wife and I saw each other naked for the first time on our wedding night, do you know what we did? WE LAUGHED! I guess you could say we were laughing *at* each other as well as *with* each other. As for myself, part of the reason why I was laughing was that I was so happy. By God's grace, I managed to remain a virgin up until that night, and the amount of peace that I felt was so overwhelming that it manifested itself in uncontrollable laughter. My wife and I experienced a lot of the emotional pleasure of sex before we experienced the physical pleasure of sex simply because we felt safe with one another, knowing that we were about to mutually give our bodies to another in the most vulnerable way possible. In fact, there was not much physical pleasure involved that night because we were so tired and exhausted from the wedding itself.

We have come so far in our sexual relationship since then that we would consider our wedding night to be the worst sex we have had together by far. Nonetheless, one of the most enjoyable aspects of marital sex is not just the physical pleasure that could technically be experienced with anyone else (which is why adultery is so rampant in our culture), but it was the emotional pleasure that originates from the special bond of being husband and wife.

There is a general understanding that sexual activities tend to be one of the highest pleasures that can be experienced in this life. After all, there are many ways that people will go to great lengths (regardless of how despicable and disgusting they are) to achieve sexual pleasure, such as sex slavery, rape, sexual abuse/harassment, pornography, child pornography, prostitution, and unfortunately that is not all of them. We can see in Scripture that God never condemns the pleasure of sex, rather He only condemns the misuse of it. Sex was meant to be pleasurable, but we will also see that the pleasure of sex is meant to point to something greater that is even more pleasurable than sex.

God saw all that He had made, and behold, it was very good (Genesis 1:31).

We have no reason to believe that the inherent physical pleasure of sex was any different before Adam and Even sinned than it was afterward when sin had spread to the rest of humanity. It is obvious that men and women both have sexual areas that have more nerve endings than the other areas on their body (penis, scrotum, clitoris), not to mention all the other pleasurable sensations of sexual intimacy (skin touching, embracing one another, oxytocin increasing throughout the body to enhance the sensitivity to the skin). There is no biblical reason to think that the physical pleasure of sex is wrong in itself, rather it was designed that way from the beginning.

1 Corinthians 7:1-5, 9 (sexual immorality)

This passage is an example of the fact that the pleasure of sex itself is never condemned in Scripture, rather it is the gross misuse of its pleasure that angers God over and over again. In this passage, Paul is admonishing Christians who are misusing the pleasure of sex in adulteress ways and is encouraging each person who has such struggles to marry so that they will not be sinning in their sexual indulgences but will have a proper relationship with a spouse to fulfill their sexual desires.

Genesis 19 (Sodom and Gomorrah)

The story of Sodom and Gomorrah is one of the most extreme examples of the misuses of the pleasures of sex. The Lord said concerning them, "The outcry of Sodom and Gomorrah is indeed great, and their sin is exceedingly grave." We see an example of their exceedingly grave sin when Lot was being hospitable to the two angels sent by God and the people were trying to break in. "Where are the men who came to you tonight? Bring them out to us that we may have relations with them." If there is any question as to what kind of "relations" they wanted to have with the angels, it is made clear when Lot, in desperation to protect the angels, offers up his virgin daughters who were already engaged to other men.

2 Samuel 11 (David and Bathsheba)

This is just one of the many passages in Scripture that involve sexual sin and is a good example of how the pleasure of sex is abused over and over again. It is not the pleasure itself that God condemns, rather it is the misuse of the pleasure. Outside of sex are many other examples of how mankind has misused something that God gave to them that was inherently good: free will in the Garden of Eden, marriage, sacrifices, offerings, the Law, etc. It is obvious that mankind was aware of the physical pleasures of sex very early on in their existence, but their gross misuse of it led to God's punishment. God is very explicit in the Law on the proper and improper uses of sexual relations.

Song of Solomon

When we speak of the pleasure-purpose of sex, it is not just referring to the physical and/or orgasmic pleasures of sex that are so often thought of in regards to sex; it also refers to the emotional pleasure that a person should experience in the mutual giving of their body to someone else in the most vulnerable way possible. The Song of Solomon is an excellent example of this as we see the engaged couple anticipating both the physical and emotional pleasures they will experience in their sexual intimacy. Obviously there is great mutual emotional pleasure as well as a sense of safety that the two have with one another.

The Pleasure-Purpose of Sex Reflects God's Character

For the LORD takes pleasure in His people; He will beautify the afflicted ones with salvation (Psalm 149:4).

But the LORD was pleased to crush Him (Jesus), putting Him to grief; if He would render Himself as a guilt offering, He will see His offspring, He will prolong His days, and the good pleasure of the LORD will prosper in His hand. As a result of the anguish of His soul, He will see it and be satisfied (Isaiah 53:10-11).

Or what woman, if she has ten silver coins and loses one coin, does not light a lamp and sweep the house and search carefully until she finds it? When she has found it, she calls together her friends and neighbors, saying, 'Rejoice with me, for I have found the coin which I had lost!' In the same way, I tell you, there is joy in the presence of the angels of God over one sinner who repents (Luke 15:10).

What brings God the most pleasure? Redeeming His

people from their sin! God has provided a way for mankind to get a glimpse of how much pleasure He takes in those who are faithful to Him and love Him. **Pleasure in sex is to reflect the pleasure that God has in redeeming His people.** The pleasure that God has in redeeming His people from their sin is something that can be seen throughout the Bible, even when God was pleased to see Jesus killed by sinners (Isa 53:10-11) so that He would be the final sacrifice needed for those who believe in Him. We also see in Luke 15:10 that even the heavens are filled with rejoicing every time a sinner repents of their sin before God.

Redeeming People from Their Sin Brings God So Much Pleasure

When God redeems sinners from their sin, they go through something called "sanctification, the lifelong process of a Christian living a life that is constantly growing in obedience to the Lord and His commands. At the end of a Christian's life, they will then be "glorified" and conformed to the image of Jesus Christ, God's Son (Romans 8:29). Ultimately, redeeming people from their sin brings God so much pleasure because the result of their redemption is being conformed to the glory of Christ Himself.

As mentioned already, the pleasure of sex is not just concerning the physical and orgasmic pleasure that can be experienced, but just as importantly it is about the emotional pleasure that two people should enjoy in willingly giving their bodies to one another in the most vulnerable way possible. The beauty of this is in the reality that many marriages will attest that their sexual intimacy will be much more physically enjoyable for one person than the other. The pleasure of sex can still be greatly celebrated in that the person who is not experiencing as much physical pleasure can still take joy in the emotional pleasure of feeling safe and comforted in the giving of their body to their spouse. In the same way, the relationship between God and His elect reflects this same reciprocation of the amount of pleasure that is enjoyed both ways. God's love is attractive to all those who receive it. In other words, there will be no one in hell who desires God's love, and there will be no one in heaven who despises God's love.

> *He will receive the crown of life which the Lord has promised to those who love Him* (James 1:12).

> *...did not God choose the poor to be rich in faith and to be heirs of the kingdom which He promised to those who love him?* (James 2:5)

> *If anyone loves Me, he will keep My word, and My Father will love him, and We will come and make Our abode with him. He who does not love Me does not keep My words* (John 14:23-24).

> *Just as the Father loved Me, I have also loved you; abide in My love* (John 15:9).

In just these few verses, we can see the mutual relationship between those whom God loves and those who love Him. The mutual pleasure that is to be experienced in sexual relationships should reflect the mutual pleasure that God and His people enjoy in the security of their relationship with Him.

One of my favorite aspects of my saving faith in Jesus Christ is that God actually wanted to save me! God had no regrets when I put my faith and trust in His Son for the salvation from the penalty of my sins. I can know this because if God had already predestined me to adoption as one of His sons by the intention of His will for His glory and grace (Ephesians 1:5), then it would not make any sense for God not to be pleased by my faith.

I believe that in the same way God has no regrets for those He has taken great pleasure in redeeming from their sins, godly sex should not be accompanied with any guilt or regret. Each time a husband and wife have sex, they should experience the same kind of joy that a believer enjoys in knowing that God is well pleased with His decision to save them!

Another aspect of the pleasure-purpose of sex is that it may also point to the pleasures that believers enjoy in Christ and the greater glory they will enjoy in heaven. There is nothing sweeter and more pleasurable for the Christian than to know they will attain a future eternal glory in heaven. If orgasmic pleasure was created to be possibly the most pleasurable physical experience that a person can enjoy during their life on earth, then imagine that pleasure being just a hint of what Christians will experience for eternity in heaven!

The pleasure-purpose of sex is to reflect the even greater pleasure that God has in redeeming His people from their sin and ultimately conforming them to the image of His Son, the second person of the Godhead, Jesus Christ.

Reflection Questions:

- How do you feel about the biblical evidence for the pleasure of sex and what it is designed to represent?
- What are some ways you think the pleasure-purpose of sex is misused in today's society?
- How do you feel that the pleasure that can be experienced from sex is a shadow of the amount of pleasure God has in redeeming His people from their sin?

5

God Is Love

Love —the L in P.L.U.M.

God is love. This is a simple foundational truth about God's character and how those who love Him should show they are truly His followers. The first of John's three letters tells us plainly in chapter 4 the sure sign of those who are the true children of God is the practice of loving our brothers and sisters in Christ.

During my first year of marriage, I heard the best way to help my wife get in the mood for sex is to do as many chores as I can around the house, buy her flowers, and then to top it off, cook her dinner. To my confusion, there were many times I did all those things, and yet my wife still wasn't in the mood to have sex. Was there something wrong with me? Was there more that I should have done to show her how much I love her? Was something wrong with her?

These questions accompanied by my failed attempts at wooing Mandy led me to bitterness and anger towards her. I would eventually begin despising her when I would see her and think to myself, *Why doesn't my wife want to have sex with me?* When trying to think of solutions to this problem, I thought maybe I wasn't communicating clearly enough with Mandy. So I asked her one night, "If I do things around the house and help you out, could we have sex tonight?"

This strategy worked a little better than the previous one,

and I thought I had the perfect solution: As long as I find something that is equal value to sex, Mandy and I could help each other out! Unfortunately, there was a big flaw to this plan—what happens when I hold up my end of the bargain and Mandy isn't able to hold up hers? There would be nights when she would get sick or not be feeling well, or our evening plans would suddenly change. These times would once again leave me feeling angry and bitter because I had come to automatically expect sex from my wife as long as I did what I was supposed to do.

Bartering for sex in marriage is not all that uncommon in marriages. Husbands will do almost anything for their wives if they can know for sure they will be getting a big reward later that evening. The danger in bargaining for sex in marriage is that in the end, it is not truly loving. Christ's love for the church is unconditional, and so should a husband's love for his wife be (and a wife's love for her husband). My question for husbands who like to barter with their wives for sex is, "Don't you think God would want you to do those nice things for your wife anyway, even if they weren't going to promise you sex in return?"

The bottom line is I was not using sex in our marriage in a way that reflected the unconditional love that God showed me through Jesus Christ dying on the cross for my sins while I was still His enemy. Once again Philippians 2:3 came to mind as God continued to convict me of my selfishness. By trying to barter for sex in my marriage, I was far more concerned with what I was receiving in return than I was about how I was serving my wife. This attitude does not reflect the love of God or the humility and selflessness of Jesus Christ to the point of death on the cross.

We can see throughout Scripture that God's people are to be loving, but also that sex is no exception. The Christian who wants to honor God through their sexuality needs to exhibit the love of God in both their abstinence from sex, as well as their partaking of this great gift as an act of worship.

I am my beloved's, and his desire is for me...there I will give you my love (Song of Solomon 7:10-12).

Song of Solomon is most famously known for its overt display of love and affection between a bride and groom. Throughout the book, the bride and groom's love for one another is driving their physical desires for one another. The dialogue between the two goes back and forth in great detail in regards to their enthrallment over each other's physical features. Their anticipation of the physical pleasure of sex is made obvious.

Genesis 29:18, "Now Jacob loved Rachel..."

This story is epic in its account of Jacob's love for Rachel. It is so strong that he agrees to work for her father, Laban, for seven years in order to marry her. The twist in the story comes when Laban swaps the other sister, Leah, in Rachel's place on the night of the wedding when the couple consummated, therefore, Jacob was contractually bound to Leah in marriage and not Rachel. Jacob then worked an additional seven years for the opportunity to marry the sister he set out to marry in the first place. We see here that the consummation act between Jacob and Leah was supposed to be out of his love for Rachel. Jacob, known as the deceiver, was deceived (maybe deception runs in the family?) himself in having sex with a woman he did not love. The feeling of betrayal must have been a strong one as he was most likely very excited about fulfilling seven years of anticipation for the day when he would finally be able to consummate his love for Rachel on their wedding night.

Thus says the Lord God, "because your lewdness was poured out and your nakedness uncovered through your harlotries with your lovers" (Ezekiel 16:36).

In this very graphic chapter of Ezekiel, one which small children were not allowed to listen to or read in the ancient Jewish culture, God uses the imagery of an unfaithful wife that turns to prostitution as to how the nation of Israel had been treating God after He had displayed His unconditional love for them. Notice how God uses the word "lovers" to describe the prostitute's clients. This usage reinforces the purpose of love in sexual intercourse and how significant it is as an act of love, even though this is an example of the gross misuse of something that is supposed to portray intimate love.

Genesis 34 (Dinah raped)

This is a tragic story where a prince named Shechem saw Dinah, the only daughter of Jacob, was deeply attracted to her and forcibly took her sexually for his own selfish pleasure. The very next verse after the rape is mentioned mentions that Shechem "loved" Dinah. Interestingly enough, the Bible does not tell us anything about Dinah's feelings about the rape or even her feelings towards Shechem. Her brothers, however, are outraged by her disgrace and end up slaughtering every male in the city (including Shechem and his father). Nonetheless, Shechem took it upon himself to have sex with Dinah in the most selfish way, all because he probably felt it was justified by his perceived love for her (or at least his definition of love). In this situation, Shechem justified his selfish act by claiming it was out of love. Even in this instance, it can be seen that sexual intimacy was understood to be a loving action.

The Love Purpose of Sex
Reflects God's Character

"Teacher, which is the great commandment in the Law?" and He said to him, "You shall love the Lord your God with all your heart, and with all your soul, and with all your mind.' This is the great and foremost commandment. The second is like it, 'You shall love your neighbor as yourself.' On these two commandments depend the whole Law and the Prophets" (Matthew 22:36-40).

Husbands, love your wives, just as Christ also loved the church and gave Himself up for her (Ephesians 5:25).

But in all these things we overwhelmingly conquer through Him who loved us. For I am convinced that neither death, nor life, nor angels, nor principalities, nor things present, nor things to come, nor powers, nor height nor depth, nor any other created thing, will be able to separate us from the love of God, which is in Christ Jesus our Lord (Romans 8:37-39).

Love is the over-arching theme of the Bible as it all points to Jesus Christ and God's great love us, and godly love is to be the primary characteristic of God's children. Above all that, God is love (1 John 4). The Apostle Paul writes in 1 Corinthians 13 about how all things spiritual are utterly meaningless if the love of God does not accompany them. It is plain and clear that God's love is to be evident in every area of the Christian's life, and sex is no different. 1 John 4:19 says, "We love because He first loved us." The Christian's love is to be a direct reflection of God's love and response to the love that He has shown through Jesus Christ. In this, we can also know that love in sex is to be a reflection of God's love for us. If we understand that God designed sex to be one of the heights of pleasurable experiences, then we can probably admit there are times when we want to use sex selfishly and would want to use it in a way that is not reflecting of God's love.

Dangers of Sex That Do Not Reflect God's Love

There are other inherent dangers in sex if it is not used in a way that reflects the love of God. One of the most extreme examples would be sexual abuse, which has existed since the days of Noah. There are biblical examples such as Lot's daughters getting their father drunk to the point where they are able to use him sexually in order to have children so they could preserve their family line (which was the origin of the Moabites), or Judah seeking out a prostitute for his sexual satisfaction with a woman he later discovered was his daughter-in-law, and God addressing the penalty for rape (stoning to death) in the law of Moses.

Sexual abuse is an extremely selfish use of sex because by definition it means having a complete disregard for the other person in the sexual act, regardless if they are consenting or not. Anytime sex is used selfishly, it is always sinful. If you have been a victim of sexual abuse, or you are currently in a relationship where someone is doing things sexually to you without your consent or desire, what they are doing is sinful, because it does not reflect the love of our heavenly Father.

Today, we have other forms of sex that do not reflect the love of God, such as friends with "benefits," pornography, pre-marital sex, and sexting. There will only be more ways of abusing God's design for sex as technological advances continue and the moral depravity of the world increases. In each of these examples, none of them express the committed and unconditional love that God expresses to His people (specifically through Jesus Christ's death and resurrection for our sins). Just as the Apostle Paul wrote about humanity in Romans 1:30, our world is full of people who are "inventors of evil." Just as love is an essential quality of living the Christian life, it is also an essential quality for sex to be used in a God-honoring way.

The love-purpose of sex is to reflect the same kind of love (unconditional, sacrificial, undying, gracious, faithful) that God has for those He has called to Himself to have eternal life.

Reflection Questions

- What are some ways you think the love-purpose of sex is misused in today's society? What do you think is the cause of this?
- If you're married, how well do you feel that the love of God is reflected in your sexual relationship? What are the attitudes and circumstances that usually lead up to the times you have sex?
- Between love and pleasure, which purpose of sex do you think is emphasized more in today's society? Why do you think this is?

6

Safety in Unity

Unity – the U in P.L.U.M.

Even in the movies and television shows, make-up sex has been portrayed to be some of the most enjoyable sex couples can experience. Little do most people know, God created make-up sex to be incredible for a much deeper and meaningful reason than for just pure pleasure.

God created the unity in sex to reflect the eternal and unbreakable bond between Him and those who love Him. As a husband and wife have sex, their physical and emotional union should reflect the fact that those who are saved through faith in Jesus Christ enjoy an eternal and unbreakable relational bond with God.

God's redeemed are "sealed for the day of redemption" as it says in Ephesians 1. It is impossible for a true believer in Jesus Christ, who has been united with God in Christ, to be separated from Him and lose their salvation.

What happens when two people have make-up sex? Make-up sex is the reconciliation of two people who were previously emotionally distant from one another. The distance and tension that two lovers feel when their relationship is not at peace is a reflection of how our sin separates us from God. The pain that a married couple experiences when they are not getting along should be a simple reminder of the pain that we should feel when we realize our need for repentance from sin. Fortunately,

God offers us redemption and reconciliation through faith in Jesus Christ!

Jesus tells a story of the rich man and Lazarus (Luke 16:19-31) that depicts the reality of just how painful it is to be separated from God for eternity. Ephesians 2 explains how Christians were all children of wrath before they were saved through their faith in Jesus Christ.

Anytime a Christian husband and wife are experiencing dissension and separation in their marriage, they can be motivated to humble themselves and seek reconciliation with one another by being reminded of how God reconciled them to Himself through their repentant faith in Jesus. It is because of Jesus that they can enjoy eternal peace with God. If their marriage is going to bring glory to the God that saved them, it needs to reflect the same reconciliation and peace that they have with Him.

The main reason God created make-up sex to be so incredible is that it is the consummation of a reconciled relationship between a husband and wife. This is the same joy that the Christian should experience upon their conversion through faith in Jesus (Luke 15:10). When a Christian makes the transition of being separated from God to being at peace with God, there is no greater joy in the world! The joy that a husband and wife feel when they have make-up sex should be a reminder to them of the joy they experienced when they "made-up" with God.

For this reason a man shall leave his father and his mother, and be joined to his wife; and they shall become one flesh (Genesis 2:24).

After God had created the first man and woman (Adam and Eve), He said in response to Adam's recognition of Eve's origin, "For this reason a man shall leave his father and his mother, and be joined to his wife; and they shall become one flesh." This certainly has to do with the sexual union the man and woman were to have with one another, and we will see confirmation of this in the next few Bible passages that quote this verse.

As Adam understood that Eve's origin came from his own body, made of his rib, the two coming together sexually signifies their bond as one flesh, even though they are two separate people.

But Jesus said to them, "Because of your hardness of heart he wrote you the commandment. But from the beginning of creation, God made them male and female. For this reason a man shall leave his father and mother, and the two shall become one flesh, so they are no longer two but one flesh" (Mark 10:5-9).

The first of three times when Genesis 2:24 is quoted in the New Testament is when Jesus was asked by the Pharisees whether or not it was lawful for a man to divorce his wife. He quotes Genesis 2:24 by stating that no man should separate what God has joined together. Jesus reaffirms the unbreakable, eternal bond that is supposed to exist between a husband and wife after they come together in sexual union.

Do you not know your bodies are members of Christ? Shall I then take away the members of Christ and make them members of a prostitute? May it never be! Or do you know that the one who joins himself to a prostitute is one body with her? For He says, "the two shall become one flesh (1 Corinthians 6:15-16).

Once again Genesis 2:24 is quoted in the New Testament, this time by the Apostle Paul. The context of the passage is referring to the sexual sin that was rampant in the church of Corinth as many were deceived into partaking in strange worship practices that involved sex with temple prostitutes. Paul is emphasizing the significance of the physical union that takes place in sexual intercourse and how it even profanes our Lord Jesus Christ when we abuse that special union.

> *So husbands ought to love their own wives as they love their bodies. He who loves his wife loves himself; for no one ever hated his own flesh, but nourishes and cherishes it, just as Christ also does for the church, because we are members of His body. FOR THIS REASON A MAN SHALL LEAVE HIS FATHER AND MOTHER AND SHALL BE JOINED TO HIS WIFE, AND THE TWO SHALL BECOME ONE FLESH. This mystery is great; but I am speaking in reference to Christ and the church* (Ephesians 5:28-32 author emphasis).

In Genesis 2:24, Paul writes about what is probably the key significance of two becoming one flesh, which is the fact that it is a picture of the unity between Christ and the church! We can see obviously that the unifying purpose of sex was specifically designed by God for His people to not only glimpse this joy within a relationship with another person, but to also be constantly reminded every time a husband and wife have sex of the much greater joy and peace that Christians enjoy in a saving faith relationship with Jesus Christ. Christians shall always be united to Christ both now and forever, and so it should be when a man and woman have sex.

> *If a man finds a girl who is a virgin, who is not engaged, and seizes her and lies with her and they are discovered, then the man who lay with her shall give to the girl's father fifty shekels of silver, and she shall become his wife because he has violated her; he cannot divorce her all his days* (Deuteronomy 22:28).

Sex was a contractually binding act between a man and a woman. This command in the Law makes it clear that even if the man and woman were not desiring marriage, the man was required to take the woman as his wife and take care of her. For a woman to be single and not a virgin would make it virtually impossible for her to marry, as men would see her as tainted and unappealing in that culture. This is where the traditionalist view in America comes from when people feel the pressure that they "have" to marry if the woman becomes pregnant out of wedlock. There are so many sad cases where two people get married only out of feeling obligated to do so, instead of because of their love and commitment to one another. Many times the relationship tragically ends in divorce not long after.

The Unifying-Purpose of Sex Reflects God's Character

For I am convinced that neither death, nor life, nor angels, nor principalities, nor things present, nor things to come, nor powers, nor height, nor depth, nor any other created thing, will be able to separate us (those whose faith is in Jesus Christ) from the love of God, which is in Christ Jesus our Lord (Romans 8:38-39).

For if we have become united with Him in the likeness of His death, certainly we shall also be in the likeness of His resurrection (Romans 6:5).

Therefore, if anyone is in Christ, he is a new creation; the old things have passed, behold, the new things have come (2 Corinthians 5:17).

Just as He chose us in Him before the foundation of the world, that we would be holy and blameless before Him. In love He predestined us to adoption as sons through Jesus Christ to Himself, according to the kind intention of His will (Ephesians 1:4-5).

How beautiful are these truths! The fact the God cannot break up with those whom He had already chosen before the foundations of the world is one of the most wonderful aspects of God's character that Christians should rejoice about. The eternal security of one's salvation is certainly something that the Israelites would not have any understanding of before Christ since the Great High Priest had yet offered His sacrifice for sins for all time (Hebrews 10:12-14).

After all, separation from God's holiness is considered to be the greatest tragedy a person can experience in both this life and the next (Revelation 20:15, Matthew 25:46, Matthew 25:30). As it was mentioned before, there is exceeding joy that is experienced amongst the angels in heaven every time a sinner repents and places their trust in God through Jesus Christ. In the story of the prodigal son in Luke 15, the great despair that the son experiences in being apart from his father's protection and provision is enough to motivate him to return home with the hopes that his father might receive him back as a lowly servant.

We see the remarkable response the father has when he sees his son returning in the distance and then proceeds to run (which would have been disgraceful for a grown man to do in that cultural setting) to him to meet him somewhere in the middle out of the excitement of being reunited with him. The joyful response doesn't stop there; the father continues the celebration by dressing the son in the finest clothes and throwing an extravagant and very costly party for him.

This story paints a vivid image of how our Father in heaven feels when a sinner repents and becomes eternally united with God through faith in Jesus Christ. This story depicts the despair one should feel when they realize their utter helplessness without God and the joy that same person should feel when they are united to God for eternity.

The unifying purpose in sex does just not represent the unity between God and His elect for unity-sake, but it also gives the Christian a much grander view of the co-eternal existence of the triune Godhead. God is defined as being love itself in 1 John 4, and for God to be eternally defined by love means that there must be a loving relationship that has eternally existed as well. For God to love, there must be a recipient of His love. We see this magnificent relationship within the Father, Son, and Spirit. The Father has always loved the Son, and the Son has always loved the Father. The unifying purpose of sex is a shadow of the unity that exists within the Godhead. The Godhead that is co-eternal, co-equal in majesty, unified in purpose, and is inseparable from one another.

The unifying purpose of sex is to reflect God's eternal, unbreakable bond He has with those who love Him. Each and every time a man and woman have sex (especially the first time), it should be with the same eternal commitment to one another that every Christian enjoys with God in their relationship with Christ.

Reflection Questions:

- How do you feel about the biblical evidence for the unity purpose of sex and what it is designed to represent?
- In what ways do you feel the unifying purpose of sex is misused in today's society?
- How do you think society would be different if people understood sex as being contractually binding for life, as they did in the Old Testament?
- If you're married, what role does the unifying purpose of sex play in your marriage? How can the unity-purpose of sex better glorify God in your relationship?

7

Multiplying What Is Good

Mandy and I were married for a year when we decided that we were ready to start having children. It all started with a conversation about how we felt about birth control. During that first year of marriage, we had no problem using condoms or birth control pills when we had sex. However, as we began to think more deeply about having children, we began to feel convicted about why we were using birth control in the first place. We asked ourselves, "If we, as Christians, worship a God who is sovereign and in control of all matters; why are we using something called birth control?" Feelings of conflict came over us as we were forced to struggle with our selfishness in wanting to have children in our own timing. We ultimately concluded that we needed to stop using all forms of birth control.

After making this decision, we, as well as all of our friends, thought that we were going to get pregnant right away. Month after month passed by with us having sex during all the optimal times of Mandy's ovulation cycle, and it eventually took a year before Mandy became pregnant. As each month passed by, we sensed an overwhelming peace in our lives, because we felt that it was just confirmation that we never should have used birth control but should have trusted God more in that He is in control of all things. We found that using birth control only gave us a false sense of control in our lives, and it left us feeling as if we had the power to decide when we would have children.

This chapter is going to challenge most people's presuppositions of the multiplying purpose of sex. By understanding the significance of the purpose of multiplying, the Christian should have a better understanding of: the purpose of having children, frequency of sex in marriage, deciding how many children to have, adoption, and more.

Genesis 1:28, Genesis 9:1, Genesis 9:7, Genesis 17:20, Genesis 28:3, Genesis 35:11, Exodus 1:7, Leviticus 26:9, Deuteronomy 7:13, Jeremiah 23:3

In each of the above passages, the words "fruitful and multiply" occur in regards to the procreation of humanity. Notice how multiplying is described as being fruitful.

Behold, children are a gift of the Lord, the fruit of the womb is a reward (Psalm 127:3).

This Psalm echoes the same message as the passages that have "fruitful and multiply"—children are a good thing! So often the potential of having children is looked at as a worrisome or risky situation, but nowhere in the Bible are children referred to negatively. Even many Christians will use birth control so that they won't have to worry about getting pregnant. It is clear from the vast array of Scripture that God designed sex for the purpose of producing more fruit in the world.

With the high rates of abortion and the lucrative industry of artificial forms of birth control, it is easy to see that one of the purposes of sex is to procreate. There is an abundance of internal evidence in the Bible as well as external evidence that we can see in within humanity.

The Multiplying Purpose of Sex Reflects God's Character

If sex was also designed to procreate, and it is somehow designed by God to reflect His holy attributes, then the question is: how does multiplying reflect God's character? We answer this question by finding in Scripture what it is that God is interested in multiplying. Let's go back and take a look at the context of all the times God says the command, "Be fruitful and multiply":

> *God blessed them (the animals), saying, "Be fruitful and multiply, and fill the waters in the seas, and let birds multiply on the earth"* (Genesis 1:22).

> *God blessed them; and God said to them (Adam and Eve), "Be fruitful and multiply and fill the earth"* (Genesis 1:28).

Both of these commands by God came after He had created everything, and it was before the first sin occurred. The significance is that God wants to see His perfect creations, unstained by the effects of sin and death, to be fruitful and multiply. As we keep in mind that these statements occur before the Fall, let's take a look at the next "Be fruitful and multiply" statements:

> *And God blessed Noah and his sons and said to them, "Be fruitful and multiply, and fill the earth"* (Genesis 9:1).

This statement comes from God immediately after the great flood subsides that wiped out all the evil. He is now commissioning Noah and his sons with the task of repopulating the earth. Why did Noah and his family survive? God tells us why:

> *Then the Lord said to Noah, "enter the ark, you and all your household, for you alone I have seen to be righteous before Me in this time"* (Genesis 7:1).

Remember how God wanted all His creation to be fruitful and multiply before the Fall occurred? Here we have a similar situation in that God has essentially instituted a hard reset on humanity, leaving the only family He considered to be righteous to survive, and gave them the responsibility to be fruitful and multiply. What is God interested in multiplying and filling the earth with? His righteousness! Noah would have likely understood full well that the reason why God killed everyone else with the flood was their wickedness in His eyes. Knowing this, Noah surely would have had a fear for himself and his own family continuing with such an overwhelming task that if their family were to behave wickedly in God's eyes, they might be killed for it. Perhaps this is why Noah cursed his son Ham when he did something dishonorable to Noah while he was asleep in his tent (Genesis 9:22).

God also said to him, "I am God Almighty; be fruitful and multiply; a nation and a company of nations shall come from you, and kings shall come forth from you" (Genesis 35:11).

Here we see more of a specific purpose of God's command to be fruitful and multiply in that He promised Jacob (whose name is being changed to Israel in this passage) that a great nation would come forth from him and his descendants. Although Jacob would have been aware of God's promise that He made with his grandfather, Abraham, and his father, Isaac, he likely would have still had a limited understanding as to what ultimately would become God's chosen nation of people. He would bless them apart from all the other nations.

Once again, God has a much greater purpose for procreation than to just fill the earth with a bunch of wicked people. He wants to fill the earth with those who love Him, those whom He has chosen as His own, the faithful remnant (Isaiah 10:20, Isaiah 37:31, Jeremiah 50:20) that the nation of Israel would come from. They would represent His righteousness through their obedience to the Law and their fear and love of the Lord.

So I will turn toward you and make you fruitful and multiply you, and I will confirm My covenant with you (Leviticus 26:9).

He will love you and bless you and multiply you; He will also bless the fruit of your womb and the fruit of your ground, your grain and your new wine and your oil, the increase of your herd and the young of your flock, in the land He swore to your forefathers to give you (Deuteronomy 7:13).

Both of these verses come in the context of God making promises to the nation of Israel as a result of their obedience to His law that He has just given them. Once again, God makes it clear that He is not interested in the earth becoming filled with more evil and ungodliness, but He is only interested in the earth being filled with those who represent His righteousness and His holiness. The nation of Israel was chosen by God to live lives that are holy and set apart from the rest of the nations (Leviticus 20:26). It was only when those people were living obediently to Him that He promised to bless them with more children.

The multiplying purpose of sex is to reflect God's own desire to grow His kingdom and His righteousness here on earth.

How Is Multiplying Referred to in the New Testament?

As we can see pretty clearly in the Old Testament, God's desire was not that humanity in general spread throughout the earth, but He desired that His elect people would be fruitful and multiply as they loved Him and obeyed His commands. They would be representatives of His holiness and His righteousness. This is the significance of the famous Psalm 23 when it says, "He guides me in the paths of righteousness for His name's sake."

In the New Testament, we see that God's desire for His people to multiply and properly represent His name does not change at all.

Go therefore and make disciples of all the nations, baptizing them in the name of the Father and the Son and the Holy Spirit, teaching them to observe all that I have commanded you (Matthew 28:19-20).

But you will receive power when the Holy Spirit has come upon you; and you shall be My witnesses both in Jerusalem, and in all Judea and Samaria, and even to the remotest parts of the earth (Acts 1:8).

Before departing to return to the heavenly Father, Jesus' last words to His disciples were that they are to multiply. In the same sense that God wanted the nation of Israel to be fruitful and multiply through their obedience to His commands, Jesus wants His disciples to be fruitful and multiply by preaching the gospel to all the nations.

The multiplying purpose of sex is to reflect God's desire to grow His kingdom. Until the day that Jesus returns and makes all things new (new heavens and new earth), God's people should be continuing to grow in righteousness. Not only is God faithful to continue to sanctify His redeemed people for His purposes (Romans 8:28-29), but there will also be a growing number of believers in the world every day until the end. God's desire is not just that people on earth would have lots of children; rather, He desires that those who have children are doing it to teach those children about what it means to love and fear God and how to know Him through faith in Jesus Christ. Only this kind of attitude towards multiplying is honoring to God.

Consider the Christian couple who considers their children as incredible blessings and gifts from God, yet they do not take

51

their responsibilities seriously in regards to teaching their children about the Lord. Are they honoring God in their child-rearing? I would argue that they are not, by the simple fact that only by their lip service are they praising God. Their neglect for their children's spiritual condition is in stark contrast to that.

There are so many examples of Christian parents who lack the understanding of what it means to be "Christian parents." While they might acknowledge how God has blessed them with children, their day-to-day lives will show that they are more concerned with: family vacations, sports, hobbies, and school. Although none of these things are inherently evil, they often prove to be idolatrous in that they tend to replace the children's spiritual development. Families will very readily skip Sunday worship services for family outings or sports events. Parents will often prioritize sports practices and homework over weekly Bible studies at home or at their local church.

God is not pleased by Christian parents having children if they are not prioritizing their children's salvation ahead of all other things in child-rearing. If Christians only enjoy their children as gifts from God and not as a responsibility for teaching them God's commands and about Jesus Christ, then unfortunately their enjoyment of those children will be in vain.

In the Old Testament law, God warns parents as to what is to become of their children if they do not adhere to the commands of the Law.

> *He who strikes his father or his mother shall surely be put to death* (Exodus 21:15).

> *He who curses his father or his mother shall surely be put to death* (Exodus 21:17).

> *If any man has a stubborn or rebellious son who will not obey his father or his mother, and when they chastise him, he will*

not even listen to them, then his father and mother shall seize him, and bring him out to the elders of his city at the gateway of his hometown. They shall say to the elders of his city, "this son of ours is stubborn and rebellious, he will not obey us, he is a glutton and a drunkard." Then all the men of his city shall stone him to death; so you shall remove the evil from your midst, and all Israel will hear of it and fear (Deuteronomy 21:18-21).

I have the feeling that the parents of the nation of Israel parented with a greater sense of fear for their children's lives than many Christian parents do. What do parents seem to be most concerned with today? I would argue that most Christian parents are more concerned for their children to be financially successful than to be spiritually mature. Christians should parent with just as much fear for their children's lives as the parents did thousands of years ago. Jesus warns us of the reality of the judgment of all people in Matthew 25, and He gives us the account of the rich man and Lazarus in Luke 16. The rich man was desperate to warn his family about the suffering he was enduring in Hades, not wanting anyone to experience the torment from which he had no escape.

The multiplying purpose of sex is to reflect God's desire to grow His kingdom. When a man and woman have sex, it should be with the commitment that if a child is a result of their sexual intimacy, they will be committed to raising that child in the Lord in the hopes that they will have eternal life through faith in Jesus Christ.

Reflection Questions

- What do you think are the most common reasons for people to want to have children?

- How would you rate the emphasis that Christian parents tend to have in personally evangelizing their children?
- How do most couples decide how many children they should have? What is the biblical support for this?
- How do most couples decide when to have children? What is the biblical support for this?

8

What All Sexual Sin
Has in Common

Now that the four purposes of sex have been established through Scripture, the next step is to observe what all sexual sin in the Bible has in common. In this chart, we see just a few examples from Scripture that expose the one thing that all sexual sin has in common. I encourage you to read through all the examples given in this chapter, as well as try to find more in the Bible that are not listed here, and see if you can find what it is they all have in common. Among the examples, there is a wide gamut of types of sexual sin. The reason I chose them is to show that regardless of how rare or how common a sexual sin is, they all have one commonality when it comes to comparing them to the four purposes of sex.

Bible passage	Topic	Pleasure	Love	Unity	Multiplying
Gen. 16:1-6	Abram, Sarai, Hagar	x			x
Gen. 19:30-38	Lot's daughters	x			
Gen. 34	Schechem rapes Dinah	x		x	
Gen. 38:12-26	Judah & Tamar		x		
Gen. 38:9-10	Onan & Tamar		x		
Exo. 22:19	Bestiality		x		
Lev. 18:22	Homosexuality		x	x?	
Deut. 22:25-27	Rape/sexual abuse	x			
Lev. 18:6-17	Incest	x		x	x?

2 Sam 11:1-6, 12:9-10	David & Bathsheba	x		
Matt. 5:27-28	Lust of the heart	x	x?	x
John 4:15-20	Woman at the well	x		
John 8:1-11	Woman caught in adultery	x		
1 Cor. 6:16-17	Sex with prostitutes	x		

Abram, Sarai, Hagar (Genesis 16:1-6)

This story is one where the Muslims will trace their ancestry back to Ishmael, the son of Abram and Hagar (Sarai's maid). In this story, Abram and Sarai grow impatient in waiting on the Lord to deliver through them the son that He had promised to Abram in chapter 15. It was Sarai's idea for Abram to have sex with her maid, Hagar, so that she would be a surrogate for Sarai. The plan worked just as they wanted it to. However, Isaac was later promised to Sarai (Genesis 17:18-19), and God made it clear to Abram (now Abraham) that the child that He was referring to in Chapter 15 was Isaac, not Ishmael, through whom his countless descendants would come from. In other words, Sarah and Abraham had made a mistake when they took matters into their own hands because they felt God's plan needed some help.

We see in this story that the only purposes of sex that were being honored were pleasure and multiplying. There is no reason to think Abram did not get any pleasure as a result of Sarai's plan (which is probably why he thought the plan was a good idea), and they thought they were fulfilling God's promise by thinking they would have the child that He promised them.

As a result of this rogue plan, they were neglecting the love and unity purposes of sex. Abram did not have sex with Hagar because he loved her, but because he loved Sarai. Although having sex with Hagar would have been a contractually binding covenant that would make Abram responsible for Hagar as a wife/concubine, his interest was not for being unified with Hagar in the same way he was with Sarai. Once again, he did it so that Sarai could say that she had a son through Hagar. We see clearly in the narrative that much tension and drama abounded in this place as Isaac and Ishmael grew up. There was bitterness between Sarai and Hagar, as well as Ishmael and Isaac. It also caused a feud between Abraham and Sarah because of the conflicted feelings Abraham had to deal with in loving one son more than the other. Through the misuse of the pleasure and multiplying purposes of sex, we can see how sex was used in a way that was selfish, harmful, and sinful.

Lot's Daughters (Gen. 19:30-38)

In this tragic story of incest, Lot and his daughters just completed a narrow escape from the destruction of Sodom. While Lot's wife was turned into a pillar of salt from turning around to see the destruction of their home, and his daughters lost their husbands-to-be in the destruction, Lot and his daughters were the only survivors among their family.

Lot's daughters were concerned that there would be no way to continue on their family without a husband, so they devised a plan to get Lot drunk and they both had sex with their father. Like most people, Lot's daughters had good intentions with their plan. But it is obvious they were aware that what they were doing was wrong because they knew Lot would not consent to such a heinous act, so they got him drunk. In today's language, it might be said that Lot was "date-raped" by his own daughters. It is not too far to assume that Lot was probably so easily made drunk because of the grievous situation he had just experienced. Not only did he lose his home, but he lost his wife and his future sons-in-law that would have taken care of his daughters and given him grandchildren.

Lot's daughters misused the pleasure, love, and unity purposes of sex. It was not pleasurable for Lot, as he was not in the right mind to consent to it. Who knows if the daughters experienced any pleasure out of it, or if they were cringing the entire time, viewing their sex act as more of a sacrifice than a pleasure. It was not reflective of the love of God, as it was a very misguided form of love that is explicitly forbidden in the Law (Leviticus 18, 20). Also, their sexual act with Lot was not for the purpose of marrying him and becoming his wife, but it was solely for the purpose of having children that would carry on their family's legacy. We can see how the neglect of the pleasure, love, and unity purposes of sex resulted in exposing itself as selfish, harmful, and sinful.

Shechem raped Dinah (Genesis 34)
Shechem, the prince of the land of Shechem, was attracted to Dinah (only daughter of Jacob), and he ended up forcefully having sex with her. He then believes that he is, in fact, in love with Dinah and demands that his father (King Hamor) get her for him as his wife. The story ends with Dinah's brothers, Simeon and Levi, slaughtering every male of Shechem for revenge and rescuing Dinah from Shechem.

In this case, the sexual sin should be obvious: rape. Rape is one of the most selfish forms of sexual conduct. It is only for the pleasure of the rapist, with a complete disregard for the victim. There is zero reflection of the love of God in rape and sexual abuse, and no desire to be eternally committed to one another (perhaps Shechem wanted to marry her, but nothing indicates that it was mutual). Lastly, Shechem probably did not have in mind raising children with Dinah from the rape incident, as the text simply says in Genesis 34:2-3, "...(he) saw her, he took her and lay with her by force. He was deeply attracted to Dinah...

Onan and Tamar (Genesis 38:9-10)

This very short story of Onan's life takes place during a very strange time in his father, Judah's life. Judah's firstborn, Er, was considered evil in the sight of the Lord and He took his life. It was then Onan's responsibility (later seen in the Law in Deuteronomy 25:5-10 and referred to by Jesus in Matthew 22:23-32) to become the husband of Er's wife, Tamar, and to have children with her as to keep Er's name alive through his descendants. Onan didn't want to have children on his brother's behalf, so when he had sex with Tamar, he spilled his sperm on the ground to not get her pregnant, and God killed Onan as a direct result of his rebelliousness.

Onan neglected the multiplying purpose of sex. While there is no reason to think he did not enjoy the pleasure of sex, we can only assume that it was also an act of love and that, due to the cultural norm of that time, he would have been prepared to take Tamar as his wife for the rest of his days. However, he denied Tamar the opportunity to have children all the while he was enjoying the sex for himself.

Judah and Tamar (Genesis 38:12-30)

Immediately after the Onan and Tamar account, the story continues with Judah sending Tamar away until he felt it was time for his third son to marry her. After that, Judah's wife passes away. Judah then sets out on a journey, and upon hearing about it, Tamar sets out to intercept him disguised as a prostitute. Tamar ends up taking advantage of Judah, as he was apparently in a sexually vulnerable state with losing his wife and then seeking out a prostitute for sexual pleasure while on his journey. The story results with Judah impregnating Tamar, and Tamar blackmailing him into becoming her new husband, thus she has a husband to take care of her for the rest of her life.

Judah and Tamar both misuse the purposes of sex in this story. Judah neglects the love, unity, and multiplying purposes of sex when he intended to go into a prostitute for the pure sexual pleasure of it. There was no expression of love, no desire to be unified with the prostitute, and he did not intend to have a child with her. Judah probably thought he would never see that prostitute again!

Tamar neglected all four of the purposes of sex, as her only intention through the whole story was to blackmail Judah to have sex with her so that he would be contractually bound to take her as a wife and be responsible for providing for her.

Bestiality (Exodus 22:19)

Bestiality is simply having sexual relations with an animal. Even if a person experiences an immense about of pleasure from having sex with an animal, it is a gross misuse of sexual pleasure, let alone the animal is not likely receiving any sexual pleasure from it. Also, there is no reflection of the love of God, there is no unification shared in the same way as it is between a man and a woman, and there is no possible way for it to result in pro-creation.

Homosexuality (Leviticus 18:22)

Homosexuality neglects the unity and multiplying purposes of sex. Even though a couple could experience just as much physical and emotional pleasure through homosexual intercourse as through heterosexual intercourse, they physiologically cannot share in the unity purpose of sex that only opposite genders can experience in sexual intercourse. Also, the form of love they are experiencing is a deceiving form of love, in that its intimate nature is misguided towards the same sex as opposed to the opposite sex. This is where the human anatomy plays its major role in sexual intimacy. Of course, homosexuality also neglects the purpose of the multiplying purpose of sex in that it is physically impossible for their sexual intercourse to result in conceiving a child. Even if a homosexual couple hypothetically wanted to adopt a child for the purposes of raising it in the Lord, it would be foundationally impossible for them to do so properly since their marital relationship does not reflect Christ and the Church from Ephesians 5.

The bottom line is, God specifically laid out the stipulation that a man shall not have sexual relations with a man, and a woman shall not have sexual relations with a woman. P.L.U.M. gives us a deeper understanding of what happens as a result of homosexuality—it misrepresents God's image in the unity and multiplying purposes of sex.

Rape/Sexual Abuse (Deuteronomy 22:25-27)

In this portion of the Law, God instructs the nation of Israel what to do in cases of the rape of a girl who is already engaged. The significance of her being engaged is that God instructed that a man who rapes a girl who is not engaged is then responsible to take her as his wife and he cannot divorce her all the days of his life. This would have served as a form of protection for a woman from being raped and then not have anyone to care for her. As for the situation for the girl that is engaged and gets raped, God makes it clear that nothing should be done to her (but only to stone the rapist to death), for she "cried out" for help, but there was no one to save her.

Rape and sexual abuse neglect all four of the purposes of sex. The only reason why "pleasure" is checked off in the chart is because the only pleasure being experienced is that of the rapist/abuser. There is no love that even remotely reflects God's love, there is no desire to be unified to the victim, and there is no desire to want to raise children with them for the Lord's sake. Rape and all forms of sexual abuse are among the most disturbing forms of sexual sin because they are done with a complete disregard of the victim's feelings.

Incest (Leviticus 18:6-17)

God lays out for the nation of Israel exactly who they can and cannot have sexual relations with. After God is done going through the entire list of who they cannot have sex with and thus marry, the only relations left are cousins. Although in modern cultures, sexual/marital relations with cousins is considered incest, it was not so in the Ancient Near East culture. God also made it clear to Israel that they are to be a nation set apart from all other nations (Leviticus 20:26), which includes the forbiddance of Israelites marrying other people groups, because it would result in incorporating false worship practices that would distract them from the one true God (Deuteronomy 7:1-4).

Of course, the laws against intercultural marriage do not apply today, as a result of Jesus commanding His followers to make disciples of all the nations (Matthew 28:19-20). Salvation was made available to all mankind by having a relationship with God as opposed to just the nation of Israel.

Incest neglects the unity purpose of sex in that it is sexual relations between people who have already been unified to a fellow family member, or it involves two family members who are a result of the same sexual union of another. God desires that a man shall leave his father and mother, and cleave to his wife (Genesis 2:24); for this to happen, that wife must be found from outside the man's father and mother.

David and Bathsheba (2 Samuel 11:1-5)

This story is probably one of the most defining moments of

David's life, right up there with his encounter with Goliath. Although while David's battle with Goliath is one of his monumental victories, his impulsive night of lustful passion with Bathsheba marks one of his biggest failures. King David, who should have been out to war with the rest of his men, chose to stay home away from the battle. Meanwhile, he spotted Bathsheba while she was bathing, sent his men to retrieve her for him, and then they had sex. Bathsheba became pregnant as a result of their sexual encounter, and then David murdered her husband, Uriah, to cover up their adulterous act.

David and Bathsheba neglected the love, unity, and multiplying purposes of sex. In their night of sexual pleasure, it did not reflect the love of God, as she was committing adultery against her husband, and David was guilty as an adulterer by having relations with a married woman. According to the law, they would have been stoned to death if they had been found out for their crime. They neglected the unity purpose of sex by having no desire to want to commit themselves to each other for life as husband and wife, and they neglected the multiplying purpose of sex in that they did not have any intention of raising a child together.

Lust of the heart (Matthew 5:27-28)

To look at someone lustfully is committing sexual sin by the fact it is committing adultery in the heart. This neglects the love, unity, and multiplying purposes of sex. It neglects the love in that there is no godly love involved in taking sexual pleasure just by looking at someone else since to look at someone does not require the consent of the person being lusted after. It neglects the unity purpose of sex in that there is no desire to want to be eternally bonded with someone, but the intention of lustful eyes is purely for a temporary pleasure. Finally, it neglects the multiplying purpose of sex in that looking lustfully at a man or woman (who is not the spouse) does not communicate any desire to want to raise children with that person, as it is once again for temporary-selfish pleasures only.

The Woman at the Well (John 5:14-18)

Jesus confronts a woman who had five husbands previous to the one she was currently with. Her multiple husbands are a good reflection of what it looks like to neglect the unity and multiplying purposes of sex. To have multiple sex partners is to neglect the unity that man and woman are to share in sex with the idea that they would not be bound to anyone else sexually. It also neglects the multiplying purpose of sex in that people who have multiple partners, moving from one to the next, show no purpose or desire to want to raise children together.

What All Sexual Sin has in Common

Do you see what all of these examples of sexual sin in the Bible have in common? They all neglect one or more of the purposes of sex. When I set out on the journey of rediscovering for myself God's purposes of sex in the Bible, I had no idea what I would find. I was really only looking for biblical solutions to the immediate issues in my marriage. However, when I took a step back and saw that every instance of sexual sin in the Bible had the one commonality of neglecting/misusing one or more of the purposes of sex. It made me wonder what would it mean for all four purposes of sex to be used properly.

The question came to my mind, "What would sex be like if it truly used all four purposes in a way that it reflected God's image properly?"If sex incorporated all four purposes, it would:

• Be full of joy (regardless of how physically pleasurable it is) because of the mutual pleasure of a husband and wife giving their bodies over to one another in complete safety and vulnerability, resting in the security of their loving relationship. Through sex, they can be reminded of the joy and great pleasures God has in redeeming them from their sins!

• Display the love of God towards one another. There would be no feelings of guilt or resentment, either before, during, or after the sex. It would not be used as a tool of manipulation or bartering between a husband and wife, and it would always be freely given of one another out of the love they have for each other.

• Strengthen the unifying bond between the husband and wife, signifying the eternal, unbreakable bond between God and those who place their trust in Jesus Christ for eternal life. Sex should always result in a husband and wife feeling more emotionally connected.

• Result in a sense of peace. There would be no worries or concern of pregnancy, understanding that God created sex to naturally result in reproduction. The husband and wife would be united in their efforts, that if their sexual intimacy resulted in a pregnancy, they would be committed to raising that child in the ways of the Lord that they might believe in Jesus Christ as well.

I ultimately concluded that when all four purposes of sex are used properly, they work together to protect the sanctity of sex, which ultimately glorifies God.

Reflection Questions:

- Are there other examples of sexual sin found in the Bible that you can think of that are not already listed here? What purposes of sex are being neglected or misused in those examples?

- What is your reaction to the one thing that all sexual sin has in common?

- How do you feel about the statement, "When all four purposes of sex are used appropriately, they work together to protect the sanctity of sex"?

- How can this view—in order for sex to correctly reflect God's image, all four purposes of sex need to be used together—be helpful for Christians to discern how to honor God with their sexuality?

Topic	Pleasure	Love	Unity	Multiplying
abortion	x	x	x	
artificial birth control	x	x	x	
friends with benefits	x	x?		
masturbation	x			
pornography	x			
premarital sex	x	x		
surrogacy				x
guilt-sex				
artificial fertility treatments				x
male sexual enhancement	x	?	?	?

9

The Purpose of Dating and Singleness

What Is the Purpose of Dating?

In my over 15 years of serving teenagers in youth ministry, some of the most common genuine questions teenagers have asked are often related to what the Bible has to say about dating and sex. Not only have I struggled over the years to give clear and biblical answers to some of these questions, but I have also heard many other youth workers struggle to give definitive answers in a culture that has strayed so far from what pleases God.

When I formulated P.L.U.M. in 2013, I found that having a much better understanding of God's design for sex is also extremely helpful as a guide for unmarried Christians in the dating world, regardless of their age.

It's important to remember that many cultures have a different view of marriage than the Bible. For the Christian, the purpose of dating should be specifically to find a husband or wife with whom to serve the Lord in their life together (1 Corinthians 7, Ephesians 5:22-33). Anything less than this is simply idolatry. If Christians were to date for any other reason, they would be subjecting themselves to inevitable sexual temptation without any ultimate goal in mind that would give them reason to remain sexually pure. Dating for any other reason would be considered idolatry because the dating relationship could potentially become more important than the Christian's relationship with God through Jesus Christ. If a Christian shows more interest in their dating relationship than their relationship with God, then there is a problem.

God's purposes of sex can only be honored within the context of a committed marital relationship that reflects Christ's relationship with the church. In dating, if the couple's goals are merely physical, then they will be committing fornication in their hearts, thus neglecting the love, unity, and multiplying purposes of sex, and only enjoying the pure pleasure of it.

If a Christian is dating someone, they need to constantly evaluate the relationship in terms of whether or not it is leading them to eventually marry. If it is not leading towards marriage, then there is no godly purpose to continue that relationship, lest they subject themselves to sexual temptations and idolatry.

Here are some of the most common questions Christian teenagers tend to have and the answers that P.L.U.M. provides:

Is dating okay in middle school and/or high school?

Once again, this all comes down to the purpose of dating. Most young teenagers in the American culture won't have any desire to get married or plan on marrying anyone they date, but they will go ahead and experiment with dating anyways. Is it possible for a 12 to 17-year-old to genuinely desire a marriage relationship through dating? Yes! However, this will simply come down to being honest concerning their reasons for dating and their spiritual maturity. It is not inherently sinful to date as a teenager. After all, most people in biblical times were getting married as teenagers (see above concerning puberty). Overall, I would hesitantly say that it is okay for a Christian teenager to date so as long as they are involving the body of Christ in a way that lovingly holds them accountable in regards to the dating process. Parents, mentors, pastors, and trusted friends should be involved in a teenager's dating life. Every Christian should seek the outside perspectives of trusted loved ones when considering entering the marriage relationship.

When should I start dating?

There are some very common reasons why people are told to wait to marry. Here are just a few of them:

• They should finish college first.

• They should be financially stable.

• They should have more life experiences first.

I don't think it is necessary to accomplish these things in order to have a successful marriage. Remember, the biblical purpose of marriage is very different from how the American culture views it. The American culture views marriage as a level of success and form of pleasure. The biblical view of marriage is an act of worship by two Christians reflecting the relationship between Christ and the Church through their commitment to one another, which is not dependent upon finances, success, age, or any other worldly gauge of maturity.

For example, the marriage relationship can very well help the husband/wife through college in their love and support of one another. It can also help them resist the sexual temptations that many single college students inevitably go through. A husband and wife who are committed to the Lord will also, in theory, have such a strong love for one another and for God that they will be motivated to apply themselves in the working world to honor the Lord through their abilities and responsibilities to one another and the church (Ephesians 4:28).

As for the "life experiences" excuse, that is simply a selfish indulgent attitude that is perpetuated in the American culture that promotes the "self" over anything else.

Christians are commanded to do "nothing out of selfish ambition" in Philippians 2, so for a Christian to dedicate time simply to enjoy the pleasures of life on their own would qualify as selfish. I would also argue that those who believe that they will enjoy those experiences more as a single person as opposed as a married person have a very low view/expectation of marriage itself. This is the kind of worldly wisdom that believes marriage to be somewhat of a hindrance to enjoying life. The Bible speaks the exact opposite of marriage.

Marriage is a gift to men and women in that when it is done biblically, it allows the husband and wife to have a greater appreciation for Christ! The marriage relationship done properly is a shadow of much greater things in heaven, namely the eternal, unbreakable, loving bond between Christ and His church.

Is it sinful to date a non-Christians?

This answer goes along with the purpose of dating for Christians. If dating should ultimately lead to a Christ-centered marriage, then how can that be possible if a Christian is dating a non-Christian? One of the biggest temptations I have seen for Christians who want to date a non-Christian is when they say things like, "he/she is so supportive of my Christian beliefs even though they aren't a Christian themselves."

Although this may be flattering, it is only temporary. Sooner or later, the Christian's biblical convictions will (or should) come to a crossroads with the non-Christian as the couple continues to make decisions concerning their relationship. At some point, no matter how supportive the non-Christian may be of the other person's Christian values, they will undoubtedly have some kind of conflict with biblical values that will cause separation in their relationship, or more likely, cause the Christian to compromise their values in an attempt to make their non-Christian partner happy (1 Corinthians 15:33).

Those Called To Remain Single

The Apostle Paul writes in 1 Corinthians 7:25-35 about his personal opinion on virgins remaining single so that they might serve the Lord with undistracted devotion. The reality is that some are called to remain single. However, pursuing lifelong singleness should not be done out of pride, spite toward the opposite sex, or bitterness of perceived failure at committed relationships. Paul lays it out clearly that the entire purpose for remaining single is to "secure undistracted devotion to the Lord." Those who feel called to remain single would be adhering to the four purposes of sex by recognizing that all sexual activity is to be preserved for the marriage relationship between a man and woman. Their lifelong abstinence would be an act of worship to the Lord, by not misusing what God created for married couples.

10

Guidance in Dating

How Far Is Too Far?

By nature of the question, most people who ask this are usually just curious how about how much they can get away with and still claim they are being sexually pure in their relationship. The more important issue here is acknowledging just how often we fall short of God's perfect standard. By keeping P.L.U.M. as the sexual standard for relationships, there is no wiggle room for any compromise. Even when a dating couple is looking at one another lustfully, then technically they have gone too far!

Within Christian dating, the most popular question remains to be "How far is too far" as it relates to physical intimacy and what is permissible in God's eyes. Before I had developed P.L.U.M. as a baseline for understanding God's design for sex and defining sexual sin, I had always been unsatisfied with the majority of the answers that were being given to this question to Christians who genuinely wanted to do what was right in God's eyes.

Many of these unsatisfying answers included ambiguous sayings, like:

- "Don't do anything you wouldn't do in front of your parents."

- "Don't do anything that you wouldn't want someone else to do with your future spouse."

- "Don't do anything that will lead to something more."

- "Don't kiss on the lips, kiss on the cheek or forehead instead."
- "Remember that God is in the room with you, and He is watching!"

Even though these types of answers are well meaning, they lack any kind of biblical support as far as defining the point of sinning sexually. As far as I can tell, the line that defines sexual sin is the same line that defines "how far is too far."

Now before you say, "Then how can anyone possibly date without sinning?" (This reminds me of when Jesus taught about marriage and divorce in Matthew 19.)

The answer is: They can't! Not that dating is sinful in itself, but it is important to realize that due to our sinful nature, no person can guard their heart and mind perfectly during the dating process. This should be just another reminder just how far we fall short of the glory of God and His holy, perfect standard.

And that's the point. It is important to remember there is no compromise with God and His standard for His people. When dating couples commit fornication in their heart by looking at each other lustfully, it should simply be a reminder to them of the dependence upon God that is required at all times. These reminders should bring us back to the remembrance of God's overflowing grace and mercy in our lives and how we are all sinners saved by grace.

There is no such thing as being completely sexually pure, even for the virgin. Everyone has fallen short of God's glory, and I am glad that God would have it no other way (Ephesians 2:8-9).

By remembering God's design for sex and how each purpose reflects His image, whenever dating couples stumble in their relationship, they will always have a baseline to look back to and remember God's perfect standard.

Each and every time any of the purposes of sex are isolated from one another, sexual sin occurs. Therefore, whenever someone lusts after another person (regardless of how far physically they are going), it is sinful and they have gone "too far." There is no such thing as anyone being completely sexually pure before marriage because just as we have all fallen short of God's glory and perfect standard, we are just as guilty sexually as well.

This is why it is so important for the Christian to be constantly humbled by the blood of Jesus Christ and just how much sin in their life has been forgiven and atoned for in order for them to have a personal relationship with the God who created them.

Instead of asking, "How far is too far," we should be asking, "What can I do to guard myself and others against temptation?"

If we understand the line for sexual sin in this way, it should help dictate the dating philosophy of a committed Christian who is seeking to honor God with their body. Here are a few practical ways this can change the way someone would date:

1. Dressing appropriately, and seeking out those who do the same

One of the biggest struggles in our culture is the custom of dressing in a way that seeks to draw the attention of other people. Christians who are seeking their future spouse should dress in a way that shows they are conscious of this and seek a wardrobe that does not intend to boast about their body. I was partially attracted to my wife Mandy when I noticed how she dressed modestly. It spoke volumes about her security in Christ. The best part is that after we got married, we got to truly enjoy each other's bodies and know that we had exclusive access to each other intimately! A man or woman who desires to reserve their bodies for their spouse should be an extremely attractive quality for a Christian.

2. Dating/hanging out in groups of Christian friends

This is one of the most practiced forms of accountability in the Christian dating community for good reason. Getting to know someone within a group setting provides several important benefits in seeking a spouse for life:

- You can see how the person treats others, both whom they get along with and those they may not.

- You can see how the other person relates to others of the opposite gender. If they are too touchy-feely or have questionable boundaries with "friends" of the opposite gender, those can be red flags to watch out for.

- The group can act as a buffer zone or even a healthy distraction that will lessen the temptation to become overly affectionate (1 Corinthians 6:18).

- Your other friends in the group can share their observations and feelings concerning the person you are dating or getting to know. Feedback from trustworthy Christian friends is extremely valuable (Proverbs 12:15). Both Mandy and I had mutual friends that thankfully had very good things to say about us to the other person as well as our relationship together, and that was one of the most significant ways that we were confirmed in our desire to marry each other.

These are just a few of the ways that dating and hanging out in groups is a healthy option for Christian dating. I'm sure there are more, and I encourage you to ask other trustworthy

Christians about some of the other benefits as opposed to the one-on-one dating method that is so much more common in the American culture.

3. Remembering where the line is

Christians should be constantly dragged back behind the line that firmly defines sexual immorality. Each time they mess up they can be reminded of the holy standard that God has set for them and also be at peace in their salvation by faith alone in Jesus Christ for the forgiveness of their sin. The Gospel tells us that we are far more sinful than we ever thought, and God is more loving than we could ever imagine. No one is pure in God's eyes, let alone sexually pure. It is only through the blood of Christ that we are purified and forgiven of our sin.

So, how far is too far? Anytime anyone looks at another person with lust, they have gone too far. Let us not compromise the holy standard that is set before us by a holy God, and to remember His great grace upon those whom He has called, we were all once children of wrath but are now made children of God through Jesus Christ.

How To Know If You Have Found the "One"

The answer to this question comes together over time. As two people start to date and get to know each other, they should be looking for signs of holiness in one another and a desire to grow continuously in their relationship with God. As parents, mentors, pastors, and trusted Christian friends are involved in the process, the couple should receive pretty clear messages as to whether or not they should continue dating and consider marriage. So often I have seen people ignore the wisdom of those who love them and want what is best for them. Those people will go on to continue in a dating relationship that is toxic and ungodly, and unfortunately, it is only a matter of time before there experience a lot of pain as a result of that unhealthy relationship. Accountability is far too underutilized in the dating realm of Christians. One cannot benefit enough from involving the outside perspectives of loved ones when considering entering the marriage relationship.

If God wants us to wait until marriage, then why did He create us to go through puberty so soon?

I have always felt that this is an excellent question for both teenager and adult Christians to have a better understanding of God's design for sex. The American culture is so far removed from the culture of the times when Jesus lived that it is far too easy to interpret God's Word through the lens of today's American culture. While keeping in mind God's four purposes of sex (Pleasure, Love, Unity, and Multiplying), here are a couple things to remember as Christians seek to honor God with their bodies.

1. The American culture does not focus on preparing young people for marriage and family, rather it focuses on preparing them to be financially and academically successful first.

In the ancient near eastern cultures of the Bible times, it was part of the culture for people at a young age to marry and work hard, which would typically be around the same time as puberty. Puberty has been for a long time a sign of physical maturity in most cultures and serves as the marker of when boys become men and girls become women.

Now compare that to our American culture, where the sign of adulthood has nothing to do with physiological changes but chronological. It has long been decided that adulthood occurs at eighteen years of age. This means that young men who complete their pubescent years before eighteen, who sound and look like grown men, are still considered minors in the eyes of the law.

The most important thing to remember concerning adulthood is that God created our bodies to be a certain way long before there were any laws or customs that men used to decide when adulthood occurs. God did not make a mistake by creating our bodies to be ready for sexual activity in our teenage years, it is the sinful nature of man that made the mistake of trying to redefine what God had already made to be good.

In other words, if you're a teenager struggling with sexual temptation and sin, don't think it is God to blame for your struggles, blame the culture you live in that does not seek God's best interest, but rather its own interests.

2. Even though God created our bodies this way, it doesn't mean everyone should get married as teenagers.

Once again, we need to remember God's four purposes for sex: Pleasure, Love, Unity, and Multiplying. Regardless of age, no one should marry and have sex without having the intention and understanding of what it means to be committed to another, the mutual sexual pleasure between a husband and wife, displaying the unconditional love of God in sex, physical and spiritual unity between a husband and wife, and raising children up to know and love God. Also, it is important to keep in mind whether or not the culture you live in prepares teenagers for such commitments or not. Just as teenagers are likely not ready for marriage, there are also plenty of adults who are not ready for marriage because of how they have been negatively affected by their surrounding culture.

Romans 12:1-2 serves as a good reminder for guidance in dating and marriage in today's American culture.

Therefore I urge you, brethren, by the mercies of God, to present your bodies a living and holy sacrifice, acceptable to God, which is your spiritual service of worship. And do not be conformed to this world, but be transformed by the renewing of your mind so that you may prove what the will of God is, that which is good and acceptable and perfect.

The bottom line for abstinence is this: Sexual sin occurs when sex is used in a way that does not reflect God's image to Him. When people have sex that does not reflect the pleasure that God has in redeeming people from their sin, His unconditional love, the unbreakable relationship between God and His people, or the committed desire to see God's kingdom grow, those people are using sex selfishly and sinfully by watering down God's perfect image. Regardless if someone is a teenager or adult, they have the same responsibility to honor God with their bodies.

11

Masturbation, Porn, and More

Is Masturbation Sinful?

Masturbation is a topic among Christians that has a wide range of answers as to whether or not it is sinful, and in what situations it is permissible. Some say it is okay for married couples to practice, some say it is okay as long as the person is not thinking lustful thoughts (which I still don't see how that is possible), and others will try to point to the supposed health benefits of masturbation because of the hormonal and chemical release that takes place that makes the person feel better afterward.

Understanding the four purposes of sex (Pleasure, Love, Unity, and Multiplying) can give the Christian a much better biblical understanding as to why masturbation is always sinful, and why it goes against God's design for sexuality.

Sexual sin occurs in the Bible each and every time the purposes of sex are used separately from one another. Masturbation is a form of sex that excludes the loving, unifying, and multiplying purposes of sex and is purely focused only on the pleasure of sex.

Masturbation for the Unmarried

As the desire for sexual activity increases through the teenage and young adult years, it is only natural for people's desire to masturbate to increase as well. It is important to remember that the same hormones that drive the desire to masturbate are the same hormones that will cause a person to look at another person lustfully, which Jesus defines as adultery in Matthew 5:27-28. Any lust for a single person is sinful, and if a person is lusting after someone (or something, AKA a fetish) for the purposes of their masturbation, then that would be sinful.

Some say they are able to masturbate without lustful thoughts. Despite my severe doubts that is truly possible, if someone is able to masturbate without lustful thoughts, I would take them back to the basic understanding of P.L.U.M., in that sexual sin occurs when God's design for sex is misused. It is important to remember that God's four purposes of sex are designed to ultimately reflect His image and to bring glory to Himself. Masturbation does not reflect God's purposes of love, unity, or multiplying.

Another side effect for those who claim to masturbate without lustful thoughts is the danger of becoming more and more desensitized to sexual stimulation that will most likely have a dramatic effect if that person were to marry. I would definitely caution someone from experimenting with masturbation without lustful thoughts because they would be endangering the health of their future sex life, which God would want that person to be able to enjoy to the fullest as a married person.

Is Masturbation Sinful in Marriage?

My wife said something to me that has always stuck with me when we had a discussion early on in our marriage on the topic of masturbation. When I asked her how she felt about the idea of me masturbating within our marriage (even if I were thinking of her when I did it), she replied, "I feel like you are leaving me out of something that I should be a part of." Her answer was profoundly wise to me, and it goes right along with the bottom line of P.L.U.M. If I were to masturbate, even while thinking of my wife, I would be excluding the unity and multiplying purposes of sex, and she would probably argue that I would be excluding the loving purpose of sex because she would not feel very loved as a result of my solo sex act.

The only form of masturbation I would argue is permissible in marriage would be mutual masturbation. It involves both individuals, they are mutually seeking the height of sexual pleasure for one another (Pleasure), they are selflessly giving of themselves for one another (Love), and they are promoting unity in their sexual relationship (Unity).

What about the multiplying purpose of sex? I believe that mutual masturbation is a biblical and God-honoring solution for birth control in marriage. It involves the married couple to mutually agree to defer to the pleasure of mutual masturbation instead of the greater pleasure of conventional sex. This can also be a helpful solution for married couples who, for some reason, may not be able to have conventional sex due to: age, disability, or injury. It's important to remember the definition of the multiplying purpose of sex: to reflect God's desire to grow His kingdom. When couples mutually agree to not have conventional sex, I believe it is a sacrifice because God designed conventional sex to be the most fulfilling kind of sex that a couple can experience. Mutual masturbation is a lesser form of married sex, and therefore it is less fulfilling. So when couples practice mutual masturbation as an alternative, they are essentially agreeing in unity to sacrifice something of greater pleasure.

Why Is Pornography Sinful?

Christians should have a much broader definition of pornography than non-Christians. Pornography for Christians is any sexually explicit image in which its purpose is to cause men and/or women to lust when looking at it (see: how far is too far?). It doesn't have to be the x-rated material anyone could easily find on the internet, but it could also be television commercials that intentionally objectify human beings for the sole purpose of increasing the chances of gaining the audience's attention. Pornography can be defined as sinful because it neglects the love, unity, and multiplying purposes of sex. Although it still includes the pleasure purpose of sex, it grossly misuses it in the sense that it is only for the pleasure of the viewer without any regard to the person that is being objectified in the image. The person in the image/video does not have any say in who gets to lust after them. Even if that person might have willingly enjoyed posing for the photos, their use of the pleasure of sex is a gross distortion of the greater pleasure that God has in redeeming His people from their sin.

LGBT Issues

The LGBT (Lesbian, Gay, Bisexual, Transgender) community will inevitably struggle with the biblical truths condemning homosexuality, gender changing, and the like. One of the ways that has helped me have civil discussions with those who support LGBT lifestyles is by using P.L.U.M. as my biblical standard. By understanding the four purposes of sex in the Bible, I am able to help others understand that sexual sin has never been determined by what culture (or Christians) considers to be weird or gross at a given time, but it is determined by any activity that does not properly reflect the image and character of God. Even though I believe it is sufficient enough to go to the places in the Bible where the LGBT lifestyle is explicitly mentioned (Leviticus 20:13, Leviticus 22:5, 1 Corinthians 6:9, 1 Timothy 1:10), it can easily seem that Christians are too often turning a blind eye to the other sexual sins (or sins in general), and only condemning the LGBT community, making the Christian community look hypocritical.

The Perceived Hierarchy of Sexual Sin

Homosexuality, sex before marriage, premarital pregnancies, pornography... for years these have been considered the big "no no's" of sexual sin in the church, and as a result we have seen a lack of grace for those who genuinely struggle with such sins. One of the clearest messages that those who struggle with sexual sin receive from the church is, "YOU'RE GOING TO HELL BECAUSE OF IT!" This truly bothers me as a Christian and a pastor for two reasons:

People don't go to hell for only certain sins, they go to hell for all their sins. In the same way, when Jesus died for our sins, He didn't just die for certain sins, He died for all our sins.

This message also portrays another false message of, "You would still be going to heaven if you didn't do that." Again, every person is a sinner who needs God's forgiveness through Jesus Christ to have eternal life in heaven.

I believe the main reason the church has developed a hierarchy of sexual sin is that the majority of Christians have lacked a full understanding of what constitutes sexual sin in God's eyes. Here is my definition of sexual sin that God has used in my own life to convict me more strictly of my own sexual sin:

Sexual sin is not defined by what we think is weird or gross, but is simply defined by anything that does not reflect God's image.

When looking at P.L.U.M. (Pleasure, Love, Unity, Multiplying) as God's design for sex, we can see in the Bible that anytime sex is referred to as sinful, at least one of these purposes of sex is neglected. By understanding how each purpose reflects God's own character, Christians can have a much fuller understanding how even sex is supposed to be an act of worship to their Creator and Savior. Here is a quick recap of what each purpose represents in God's character:

Pleasure: pleasure in sex is to reflect the pleasure that God has in redeeming His people from their sin (Luke 15:10, Psalm 149, Isaiah 53:10-11).

Love: love in sex is to reflect God's unconditional and immense love for His people (Matthew 22:36-40, Ephesians 5:25-28, Romans 5:8, John 13:34-35).

Unity: unity in sex is to reflect the eternal and unbreakable relationship covenant between God and His people (Genesis 2:24, Mark 10:5-9, 1 Corinthians 6:15-16, Ephesians 5:31-32, Romans 8:38-39).

Multiplying: multiplying in sex is to reflect God's desire to grow His kingdom (Genesis 1:28, Deuteronomy 6:6-9, Matthew 28:19-20).

The conclusion I come to about sexual sin is this: Sexual sin occurs anytime someone separates any of the four purposes of sex from the others. Yes, this will most likely significantly limit what most well-meaning Christian marriages are already practicing who believe they are already honoring God in their sex life, but that's the point!

God is a holy and perfect God, and it should not surprise Christians to learn that there is more sin in their life than they originally believed, especially if they are growing Christians.

This destroys the hierarchy of sexual sin that should never have existed in the church in the first place, and it rightfully explains how ALL SEXUAL sin is disgusting in God's eyes. When Jesus teaches about the lust of the eyes towards another human being is just as sinful as the physical act of adulterous sex, He is saying very clearly "all sexual sin is disgusting in God's eyes."

Here are three important reasons why the church must destroy the hierarchy of sexual sin:

- It will make each person more aware of their own sinfulness and hopefully will also make them more aware of God's grace and forgiveness towards them when they place their faith in Jesus Christ.

- It should significantly enhance the Christian's ability to show grace and mercy towards those who struggle with a different sexual sin than they do, realizing God shows the same grace to one repentant sinner as the next regardless of what their sins are.

- It has allowed Christians to push the boundaries of sexually sinful behavior and to ignore the seriousness of all sexual sin. It can also lead to a sinful judgmental attitude towards those who have committed the "big ones" from those who have not.

By God's grace, I was able to remain a virgin until I got married at 25 years old, but I was far from being sexually pure. I was badly damaged from my battles with pornography and lust as a teenager. The hierarchy of sexual sin is harmful to the Christian community because it does two things:

First, it creates an environment of pride for those who believe they have maintained more sexual purity than others by not committing the "big ones" (premarital sex, teen pregnancy, homosexuality). And second, it has caused many who have struggled or committed some of the "big ones" to struggle with unnecessary feelings of rejection by the church or Christian communities, even if they are seeking help.

I feel very strongly about destroying the hierarchy of sexual sin because Ephesians 5:3 makes it clear that there should not even be a hint of immorality among Christians. Each Christian needs to first realize the seriousness of their own sin before they can go and help another with their sin (Matthew 7:3-5). I thank God for continuing to help me see more clearly my sinfulness because it is only since then that I can see more clearly His love, mercy, and grace!

12

P.L.U.M. for marriage

Idolatry of sex in marriage

You shall not make for yourself an idol, or any likeness of what is in heaven above or on the earth beneath or in the water under the earth (Exodus 20:4 NASB).

"If God were to remove sex from my marriage, would I still love my wife as Christ loves the Church?" This was a question that I had asked myself in the first year of my marriage. It came during a humbling time of prayer and Bible study after Mandy and I had a heated argument about sex. I was the one with the much stronger sex drive in our marriage, and it seemed that in our first year together, I was always discontent with how often we had sex. We knew that we were not alone in this struggle of intimacy in marriage.

When I went to the Scriptures to gain understanding, two of the passages God led me to were Ephesians 5:22-33 and Philippians 2:1-8. Both of these passages are a very distinct picture of God's love displayed to His people through Jesus Christ. The Ephesians passage is all about how marriage is to function: how a wife is to love her husband, and how a husband is to love his wife. The Philippians passage speaks of the humility and selflessness of Christ, and how He is the model for selfless living.

Two specific verses, in particular, jumped out to me as I was still cooling off from the argument that Mandy and I just had:

Ephesians 5:25 "Husbands, love your wives as Christ loved the church and gave Himself up for her" and Philippians 2:3 "Do nothing out of selfish ambition or vain conceit, but with humility of mind regard one another as more important than yourselves."

It was at this point when the question came to my mind, "Corwin, if God were to remove sex from your marriage, would you still love your wife as Christ loved the Church?"

I was immediately convicted of my selfishness and my lack of willingness to love my wife as Christ loves the Church. Most Christian marriage books and blogs are very good about talking about the importance of having sex in marriage and all the joys that come with it. However, something that I had never seen in any Christian marriage literature is dealing with the potential of God removing sex from the marriage.

There are several ways God may remove sex from a marriage, whether temporarily or permanently: injury, illness, pregnancy, age, or physical separation.

One of the ways that God has blessed our marriage is by showing us how periods of abstinence could be used as very healthy tools in strengthening our marriage. These periods exposed just how much we (more me than Mandy) had idolized sex in marriage. God used these periods of abstinence to grow me in selflessness towards my wife and to rely on Him more to be the primary source of my fulfillment. I also increased in the ways that I sought to love my wife and to express my love for her in other ways than just sex.

I believe it is very common for Christian marriages to idolize sex. The influence of the sinful American culture and its sinful view of sex has no doubt infiltrated the Christian culture and its biblical views. Most Christian marriages in America have more of a worldly perspective of sex rather than a biblical one. This is also the reason why the Church in America is struggling so much on current issues such as abortion, homosexuality, LGBT, birth control, childbearing, pornography, and premarital sex.

Sex is certainly idolized in the American culture (and others as well, but I have only lived in America), and that has certainly taken its toll on the average Christian living in America. As a result, I believe it is very likely that many Christian marriages probably idolize sex without even realizing it. Almost all Christian marriage books and blogs are all about how to have more and more sex, and how to enjoy it to its fullest. I am not against having a high frequency of sex in marriage and certainly not against enjoying it to its fullest, but I do believe that Christians must be careful in treating sex in marriage as if it will always be there.

Just as God allowed Satan to work in Job's life, there is nothing that is off-limits when it comes to losing what is valuable to us to bring God more glory. Sex can very much be one of those things that can be removed from marriage, and yet the command for husbands and wives to continue to love each other still remains.

If you are currently married and are having lots of sex, very little sex, or maybe God has removed sex from your marriage for whatever reason, I'd like to leave you with two questions to ponder:

1. If God were to remove sex from your marriage, would you still love your spouse as God commands husbands and wives to love one another?

2. If God were to remove sex from your marriage, would you love the Lord your God with all your heart, soul, mind, and strength?

Can I Barter for Sex with My Wife?

Bartering for sex looks something like this: "Hey honey, if I do all the housework and laundry for you, can we have sex tonight?" or "Hey baby, it's my birthday! That means we are having sex tonight!" (with the attitude that it would be completely wrong to NOT have sex on my birthday).

Although this can begin very innocently and effectively, I want to warn all marriages against viewing this as an acceptable form of sexual intimacy in marriage. Two inherently sinful issues need to be addressed in these situations:

1. It's selfish

Do nothing out of selfishness or vain conceit, but with humility of mind regard one another better than yourselves (Philippians 2:3).

Jesus Christ is our example of selflessness.

It is very unhealthy for marriages to perform on a 50/50 basis. The worldly sinful view of marriage would have us believe that the husband should only put in as much as the wife does, and vice versa; otherwise it's not "fair." The biblical view of marriage is 100/100, that means the husband is fully devoted to his wife regardless of her apparent devotion and vice versa. When a husband and wife are fully devoted to their service to God as husbands and wives, there should be no concern about whether or not the other spouse is fulfilling their responsibility or not. Christians should marry other Christians so that they have the same biblical expectations of each other.

When a husband (it's usually the husband that does this) does household chores or favors for the wife only in order to receive sex in return, it is putting a price tag on sex and making it a conditional form of love. Husbands should be offering to do more housework regardless of whether or not their wives will have sex with them in return. The moment a marriage makes sex conditional, it sets itself up for future problems when the conditions aren't met for some reason.

Having conditional sex will also set a bad precedent for sex in the future. When sex doesn't happen, it conditions the husband to think, "She will only have sex with me if I work for it."

2. It's not loving.

> *"This is My commandment, that you love one another, just as I have loved you"* (John 15:12 (Jesus' Olivet discourse).

The four purposes of sex (pleasure, love, unity, multiplying) should always be used together anytime and every time two people have sex. It is the four purposes that protect the sanctity of sex and prevents it from being used sinfully, selfishly, or harmfully. Bartering for sex is not loving. At least, it does not reflect the kind of godly love that we see in the Bible. God's love is unconditional, faithful, enduring, everlasting, and self-sacrificing. Once again, anything that a husband would be willing to do for his wife to have sex with him, HE SHOULD BE DOING ANYWAY, solely out of the love that he has for her. A husband (or wife) should not put conditions on their loving affection for one another but rather allow their unconditional service to each other be the drive of their sexual desire for one another.

Our Story

There was a time when I thought bartering for sex was healthy for our marriage (this was during our first year of marriage). It seemed that it was making me a better husband! After all, I was doing more chores around the house and being more helpful, and in return, my wife would have sex with me. It felt like a win-win situation! However, inevitably there would be times when factors outside of our control would affect the outcome of whether or not the sex part happened. For example, she might have been affected by her menstrual period, our evenings ran late, or we might have gotten into an argument that ruined the mood.

I was convicted that our sex life was not based on our love for one another, but rather it was based on my love for myself. Even though I truly loved my wife, the truth was that the sex was more about me than it was about us. Putting an end to bartering for sex in our marriage only improved how I actively loved my wife. House chores became a regular duty of mine as a way to serve my wife, instead of a way to get something in return. We were also able to have romantic evenings together without the tension of whether or not it was going to end with sex, which freed us both up to feel more relaxed when we spent time together.

I can still remember the excitement and anticipation of enjoying sex for the first time after we had gotten married. As a result, I was looking forward to enjoying the splendors of sex with my wife with reckless abandon! My drive for sex was more about my excitement for it than it was about enjoying it with my wife. I think most Christian men and women are not properly prepared for the responsibility of having sex when they get married, simply because they are only focused on the pure pleasure of it, and not on the other three biblical purposes of sex.

I encourage all Christian husbands and wives not to barter for sex in their marriage and thus avoid from it becoming an idol in their marriage. Wives, protect your husband's hearts by not giving in to his requests to barter with you for sex. Husbands, love your wives as Christ loved the church and serve her selflessly and completely without placing conditions on your acts of loving kindness towards her.

Demanding Sex in Marriage

One of the most common struggles in Christian marriages is the expectation of how often a husband and wife should be having sex. Most of the time it is the husband who is desiring more sex than the wife, but there are also many cases where it is the opposite. For this section, I am going to focus on the husbands who tend to want sex more often than their wives do.

Probably the most quoted verse in the Bible when it comes to discussions about how often married couples should have sex is 1 Corinthians 7:5:

Stop depriving one another, except by agreement for a time, so that you may devote yourselves to prayer, and come together again so that Satan will not tempt you because of your lack of self-control.

Husbands will often point to this verse to tell their wives not to deprive them sexually or else they will fall into temptation and sin sexually, whether it be through masturbation, pornography, or even physical adultery with another woman. As a result, this verse has also been used many times to instill fear and guilt in those wives that if they don't put out sexually for their husbands as much as they want, then they will be the cause of the downfall of their marriages. THIS IS WRONG.

Here are a few things those husbands forget to consider:

1. The "lack of self-control" is a bad thing.

The Apostle Paul urged the Corinthians to not neglect one another because sexual immorality was already very prominent among them, and they were lacking self-control. Lacking self-control is not an excuse, but rather it is a deficiency in the Christian life that needs to become more and more evident as one matures in their faith. Galatians 5:22 spells it out very clearly that self-control should be something that Christians are constantly growing in, and that sensuality (a lack of sexual boundaries) in Galatians 5:21 is something to steer away from.

Husbands should not be content in their lack of self-control or be using that as a reason why they feel they need to have sex a certain number of times per week or month (or per day!). To lack self-control is a bad thing, and to be continually growing in self-control is evidence of a mature Christian.

2. "Love" is one of God's purposes of sex.

To bring this back to God's four purposes of sex (Pleasure, Love, Unity, Multiplying), Husbands should never rely on guilt to convince their wives to have sex with them. If a wife is having sex out of guilt and not out of feeling dearly loved and valued by her husband, then the husband needs to think of a different strategy. Dr. Eggerichs, author of *Love and Respect*, mentioned in his podcast how he has counseled many women who regularly are secretly in tears just moments before having sex with their husbands, all because of the overwhelming guilt they experience from their husbands demanding sex from them.

In Ephesians 5:25-29, husbands are commanded to love their wives as Christ loved the church when He gave Himself up for her by dying on the cross for our sins. Selflessness and servanthood are two main characteristics of the love of Jesus, and this same love needs to be shown in the area of sex in marriage. Husbands, if you need guilt and shame to talk your wife into having sex with you, then you're doing it all wrong!

By the way, one of the reasons why make-up sex tends to be some of the most exhilarating and satisfying sex in marriage is because of the renewed sense of love and unity that is experienced leading up to it that brings a couple back together physically and emotionally after they felt distant from one another.

3. Sex is not a "need" but rather another way for God's image to be properly reflected in marriages.

In Matthew 19, after Jesus had given His teaching on divorce, the disciples responded by saying, "If the relationship of the man with his wife is like this, it is better not to marry."

Jesus then replied,

> *Not all men can accept this statement, but only those to whom it has been given. For there are eunuchs who were born that way from their mother's womb; and there are eunuchs who were made eunuchs by men; and there are also eunuchs who made themselves eunuchs for the sake of the kingdom of heaven. He who is able to accept this, let him accept it.*

In other words, Jesus is saying that men don't need sex to live a godly life. After all, Jesus lived as a sinless human being for 33 years as a single man and was tempted in every way we are, yet was without sin (Hebrews 4:15). Even the Apostle Paul encouraged other men to live as he did as a single man so that their devotion to God would not be challenged (1 Corinthians 7). However, Paul also says that the single lifestyle is not for everyone but only those who are chosen for it.

The bottom line is sex is not a physical need for men or women to live an obedient lifestyle to God. Men who fear falling into sexual temptation because of not having sex as frequently as they desire need to grow in their self-control and evaluate the accountability they have in their life to help them avoid sinning sexually.

God gave us sex as another way to properly understand and

reflect His perfect image. When sex is used in a way that does not reflect the pleasure God has in redeeming His people from their sin, the unconditional love He shows to His people, the unbreakable-eternal relationship between God and His people, and God's desire to grow His kingdom, then it is being used selfishly and sinfully.

I encourage all husbands and wives to consider using P.L.U.M. as a standard of how they go about their sex lives, and experience how using sex according to Pleasure, Love, Unity, and Multiplying can bless their lives and marriages in growing them in their faith in Jesus Christ.

Birth Control

"We will have_____# of children and start when we are _____ (ready, financially secure, done travelling, satisfied with our married-with-no kids years, married ____# of years, etc)."

Sound familiar? It should because this conversation probably happens during or before every marriage. Starting a family, let alone getting married, can be extremely intimidating especially when considering the impact it could have on the couple financially, relationally, physically, and more.

As a result, most couples will use birth control to be able to have sex without having to worry about getting pregnant until they believe they are ready to start a family. There is an inherent problem with this sort of thinking, which first came from the world and has invaded its way into the Christian culture. The inherent issue is that the use of artificial birth control and fertility treatments are inherently selfish. They are a way of saying, "I want to be in control of what I want and when it happens."

Grief should never be associated with pregnancies.

The multiplying purpose in sex is meant to reflect God's desire to multiply His kingdom and the joy that is experienced in the heavens each and every time one sinner repents (Luke 15:10). In the same way, every pregnancy (new life) should be met with the same kind of joy that occurs in heaven when a sinner is born again into the kingdom of God. For those who use birth control, they will undoubtedly have to go through some kind of grieving process if they were to get pregnant when they thought they were doing what was necessary to prevent pregnancy. I believe using artificial forms of birth control and fertility treatments are inherently selfish because it is attempting to assume control over our bodies and setting the individual up for failure when they are forced to grieve when their plan does not go accordingly.

With God, all things are possible.

After hundreds of years without the Israelites hearing from a prophet of God, God's word returned emphatically with two miraculous events showing that indeed all things are possible with Him. The first was answering the prayer of Zacharias and Elizabeth (Luke 1:5-24), who were well past childbearing years. God blessed them with their first child through the conception of John the Baptist. The second one, on the other side of the childbearing spectrum, happened soon after God had spoken to Mary and Joseph (Luke 1:26-38) and let them know that Mary would be the virgin mother of Jesus, the Savior of the world. Remembering that nothing is impossible with God should prevent the Christian from having a false sense of control over their life, even their own bodies. God's will cannot be thwarted by any means of birth control and He can make it possible for any woman to have a child at any age if He desires.

Christians should be encouraged by the patience of Zacharias and Elizabeth and how they remained faithful to God even in the midst of their struggles to conceive a child. Many people today would often doubt God's goodness if they were to go through similar situations.

Just because it works, it doesn't make it right.

I have heard many Christians praise God for seeming to provide them the ways they desired when it came to using artificial fertility treatments to conceive a child. However, I believe Christians should be very cautious about discerning God's will based on whether their ideas worked or not.

After seeing Sodom destroyed, and only Lot and his two daughters survived, his daughters had the idea that they could continue their family bloodline by getting their father drunk (while he was probably in shock and depression from losing his wife and hiding in a cave with his daughters) and having sex with him so that they can have his children. Although the Bible does not explicitly say this was wrong, we can know from the rest of the Bible that God would not have approved of this. However, IT WORKED! The daughters would have most likely felt assured that they had done the right thing in God's eyes simply on the basis that their plan worked and would have been under the impression that God had blessed them and their efforts to save their family heritage (Genesis 19:30-38).

Abram and Sarai were told by God that they would finally have their first child even in their old age. Sarai waited ten years after they had received this message and she was 75 years old when she decided she was done waiting on the Lord to fulfill the promise. She shared her idea with her husband Abram that he should have sex with their servant, Hagar, and have the child that God had promised them through her. Guess what...IT

WORKED! Sarai would have been under the impression that God had indeed blessed their decision as being the right one solely on the basis that their plan had resulted in exactly what they desired. However, we can see by the way the relationships were torn apart by the jealousy that ensued afterward between Sarai and Hagar that it wasn't such a good idea. Another thirteen years later, God told Abram (now Abraham) that the child He was going to bless him with was going to be conceived by Sarai (now Sarah) within the next year (Sarah was 99 years old at Isaac's birth). Abraham was confused and had thought that Ishmael (the first son) was the one God had originally spoken of but was then corrected that it would indeed be Isaac, the first son of Sarah and Abraham.

These are only two of the many examples in the Bible to prove that just because someone gets what they want, it doesn't mean that it was right. God allows us to sin every single day and does not prevent us from making sinful decisions. He does, of course, use all things ultimately for His glory despite how sinful we are, and for that, we should be thankful.

If one is to apply the principles of P.L.U.M. consistently, then the conclusion is that Christians should not use artificial forms of fertility treatments because as soon as they go outside of the natural means of a husband and wife conceiving a child the natural way, they will begin going down a slippery slope where it will not be clear just how far they should go. P.L.U.M. guides Christians to limit themselves to either conceiving children naturally or choosing adoption if they want to have children.

The four purposes of sex (pleasure, love, unity, multiplying) is a beautiful structure designed by God, and when used properly, actually protects the sanctity of sex and aims to keep what is holy, holy. When two people have sex according to its four purposes, it prevents them from misusing it in a way that is self-seeking, sinful, and harmful.

There are several reasons people will choose to use artificial fertility treatments. To postpone childbearing during prime career years and struggling to conceive naturally are probably the most common ones. I understand there are many good-willed, Christ-loving couples out there who are currently struggling with conceiving a child that they so dearly desire. My encouragement to them is to wait patiently on the Lord and to pray seriously about whether or not there is any selfishness in their desire to have a child. As the multiplying purpose in sex reflects God's desire to grow His kingdom, the one biblical reason for having children is to raise them up in the Lord so that they might fear Him, love Him, and enjoy Him forever. All other reasons for having children simply fall short of what God ultimately desires for them. I believe that those who cannot conceive naturally but want a child as soon as possible should either be patient and wait to see what the Lord has for them or pursue adoption. Many children need to be adopted, and even more, they need to be taught the good news of Jesus Christ. As Christians, we must be willing to confront the selfishness that naturally exists in us that tells us that we deserve to have children from our bodies, no matter the cost. God has much greater purposes for having children, and we need to hold His purposes above our own.

Concerning birth control, the worldly view of sex has so invaded the Christian culture that Christian men and women are under the impression that sex is to be enjoyed as much as possible and without self-control. Birth control is what makes it possible for two people to have sex as much as they want without feeling like they are "risking" getting pregnant (which is in opposition to the multiplying purpose of sex). In 1

Corinthians 7, the apostle Paul is writing to the church about how their lack of self-control is causing them to fall into sexual sin. Many people will read this passage and interpret it to mean that those who struggle with sexual sin should get married so that they can have sex whenever they want. However, Paul points out that it is their lack of self-control that is the root of the problem. Galatians 5 lists self-control as part of the fruit of the Spirit, so we can know that to lack self-control as a Christian is a bad thing.

I am convinced that most Christians (mostly men) today are more in the habit of feeding their lack of self-control in sex rather than practicing it.

The use of birth control perpetuates the notion that we should be available for sex at all times, just for the pure pleasure of it. It also sets people up for potential disappointment and grief if they were to get pregnant despite their efforts in trying to prevent pregnancy. As I have already established, those are reactions that should never be associated with pregnancy. Eliminating unwanted pregnancies would also eliminate the temptation of abortion, child abandonment, and couples splitting up because they were not ready to raise a child together.

So what is the alternative to using artificial forms of birth control?

Sex should be practiced in faith

God created us, male and female, in His image to glorify Him. When He saw all that He created, it was very good. God established a natural form of birth control in the way of the woman's ovulation cycle. This form of natural birth control is one that requires faith each and every time two people have sex and promotes the use of self-control in the frequency of sex. Even when two people have sex when the woman is not ovulating or fertile, they should do so while acknowledging that nothing is impossible with God and that their sex can still result in pregnancy if the Lord wills. This view of sex is completely counter-cultural, where the world would have us believe that we should be able to have sex as much as we desire. Both sex and abstinence should be practice in faith in humbling ourselves to God's authority and will in our lives. If men and women went into every sexual encounter with the mutual commitment to potentially raise a child together as a result of them having sex, there would be no "unwanted" pregnancies and 99% of the nearly 1 million abortions in America annually would not even exist. The other 1% of abortions are of women who are raped, which is non-consensual. I am focusing primarily on those who have consensual sex and get pregnant.

The Big Picture

Do you see God's beautiful structure of accountability in His four purposes of sex (pleasure, love, unity, multiplying)? I pray that you do not see God's purposes for sex as an unreasonably strict standard but rather a guide on how to have a kind of sex life that is described by selflessness and holiness. God's purposes for sex are designed to protect the sanctity of sex and to keep what is holy, holy. Whenever all four purposes of sex are being honored between a man and a woman, they work together to protect the sanctity of sex.

I want to propose that all Christians practice something that James wrote to the church in his New Testament letter:

> Come now, you who say, "Today or tomorrow we will go to such and such a city, and spend a year there and engage in business and make a profit." Yet you do not know what your life will be like tomorrow. You are just a vapor that appears for a

little while and then vanishes away. Instead, you out to say, 'If the Lord wills, we will live and also do this or that.' But as it is, you boast in your arrogance; all such boasting is evil. Therefore, to one who knows the right thing to do and does not do it, to him it is sin (James 4:13-17).

When it comes to family planning, let us say...

"If the Lord wills, we will have ____# of children and start when we are _____ (ready, financially secure, done travelling, satisfied with our married-with-no kids years, married _____# of years, etc)."

How This Has Blessed My Marriage

Mandy and I started off like most marriages, using birth control so that we could begin our "sexual journey" together by enjoying one another. We became convicted of our selfishness in using various birth control methods about a year into our marriage. We asked ourselves, "If we believe in a God that is in control of all things, then why are we trying to dictate our marriage with birth 'control'?" Also, Mandy experienced all kind of undesirable side effects from birth control, which was confirmation to us that what we were doing was not honoring to God.

When we made this decision, we shared it with our friends. Sure enough, they all said things like, "She's going to be pregnant next month." (It usually was said with a negative tone, as if pregnancy is a bad thing.) It took over a year for us to conceive our first child, and during that time as each month went by, our faith grew stronger in confirmation that God is indeed in control.

God has transformed me as a husband in the way of teaching me just how much self-control I was lacking in our marriage when it came to sex. I had grown up with the view that sex in marriage is mostly for husbands because we have a stronger desire for sex (in most cases). I was under the assumption that if I was horny, then my wife needed to help me fix it. Philippians 2:3 says, "

Do nothing out of selfishness or vain conceit, but with humility of mind regard one another as more important than yourselves.

This verse changed my marriage because ultimately it changed me. I came to realize just how selfish my view of sex was. I expected Mandy to be ready to have sex anytime I was, and if she weren't ready, then I would guilt her for it.

I thank God every day in the way He has made me more selfless in my views of sex and what my perceived sexual needs are. His light exposed the sinfulness in my life where I allowed my ability to love my wife to be hindered when we didn't have sex as often as I thought we should. In reading Scripture, I see how godly love endures all things without wavering in commitment. When the time comes when sex is removed from our marriage completely, I want to be able to say in that day, "That's okay, because the foundation of our marriage has been our commitment to Christ, not our commitment to sex." In other words, every marriage will reach the point where sex won't be realistic anymore, and it is better to be prepared for that day ahead of time, rather than wait until it happens to grieve the "loss of sex."

Once again, God has blessed my marriage through our convictions from His Word. Although it can be difficult at times, we have a peace that we are living obediently to God's Word and that He is continuing to shape us and mold us to the image of His Son, who was obedient to the point of death on the cross.

In our pre-marital counseling sessions, we talked a bit about birth control and how we were planning on using it in the beginning of our marriage, because all the advice we were getting from older married couples was, "get to know each other sexually and enjoy it before having kids."

This sounded like very good advice at the time. However, as the topic of our sex life dominated our arguments during the first year of marriage, we were far from enjoying one another sexually. We were trying to answer a variety of questions at the same time, such as:

• Why is Mandy's body reacting strangely to the birth control pills?

• Should we only use condoms?

• When is the right time to try to have our first child?

Ultimately, we were finally confronted with the question, "If we claim to be individuals who worship a God that is in complete control of all circumstances, and we are supposedly submitting our lives to Him, why are we using something in our lives with the word "control" in it?

The conviction came quickly after the question was asked. It was that same week we decided to go completely off artificial forms of birth control and submit that area of our lives to whatever God wanted for us. Many of our friends responded afterward by saying things like, "You're going to get pregnant next month!"

Month after month went by for the next 12 months, and Mandy was not pregnant. As each month went by, our faith grew more in knowing just how much God was in control of the entire situation. From that point on, Mandy and I have been free from the use of any form of artificial birth control, and we have been at peace knowing that God ultimately rules over our bodies (1 Corinthians 6:19).

We are now practitioners of the "Rhythm Method," meaning that our form of birth-control is centered around

Mandy's monthly cycle and practicing self-control in the times we abstain and the times we have sex.

As a man who grew up in a culture where self-control is not taught, especially in the area of sexual activity, I cannot be thankful enough for how God has grown me more into the image of Christ from this conviction of practicing self-control in marital sex. When we were first married, I had an extremely selfish view of sex, that somehow it was all about me and meeting my "needs." As I continued to study God's Word through the difficult times of our marriage, it became more and more apparent to me that the idea of "sexual needs" as a man is all a lie that our culture has led many Christian men to believe.

In Matthew 19, Jesus gives the difficult teaching about how divorce was never God's will for marriage. The disciples followed up with the statement, "It's better not to marry!" Jesus then goes on to explain that some men are equipped by God to remain celibate for their entire life even though they could very well be married and sexually active.

In 1 Corinthians 7, Paul's personal opinion to single or widowed people is to remain single if at all possible to have an undistracted devotion to the Lord. At the same time, he encourages those who are burning with passion to go ahead and marry so that they do not succumb to sexual sin in their lack of self-control.

The main focus of these two chapters about sex and marriage is that men (and women) do not have a legitimate need for sex to live God-honoring lives. As Christians, we are to practice self-control and reliance upon Jesus Christ for all the things we are called to do as followers of Jesus. Philippians 4:13 "I can do all things through Christ who strengthens me" is in the immediate context of the Apostle Paul explaining his contentment in all situations that is only made possible through Christ.

I would like to remind my readers of a question that I had to answer in my own marriage: If God were to remove sex from your marriage, would you still be able to love your spouse the way God commands a husband and wife to love one another (Ephesians 5)?

At the time I asked myself this question, my answer was, sadly, no. It was at this moment that I knew that the sin I was looking for was not on my wife's part but my own. This is how God convicted me of having a selfish view of marital sex. I was immediately reminded of Philippians 2:3, that NOTHING should be done out of selfishness, and that includes sex in marriage.

Frequency of sex in marriage

Many times Christians will question my view of birth control by using 1 Corinthians 7:1-5 as a way of saying, "use of artificial birth control is necessary for husbands and wives to be as sexually active as needed, lest they fall into adultery." However, the key words at the end of that passage are self-control. The reason Paul was telling the husbands and wives not to neglect one another sexually is because they lacked self-control. However, we can know self-control is supposed to be an evident and growing component of the Christian life (Galatians 5—the Fruit of the Spirit).

For husbands and wives that are concerned with sex becoming less frequent in their marriage, I first want to encourage them that the practice of self-control is something that God desires from all those who love Him.

Also, ask yourselves, "What ways has our culture affected our view of sex in marriage and how does that compare to what the Bible has to say about sex and marriage?"

Abstinence in marriage

Probably one of the most controversial statements I will make in this book is: Abstinence in marriage should be practiced if the couple does not want to conceive children.

This goes along with the notion that sex is often idolized in marriage, and that our human nature will want to enjoy sex even if it is by selfish means. For married couples who do not want to conceive children, I would encourage them to consider forgoing the pleasure, love, and unity of sex so that they can continue to protect the sanctity of the multiplying purpose of sex. There are many other ways to express sexual desire for each other besides sexual intercourse, such as various forms of mutual erotic touching.

It is a long-held belief that sex is required to have a healthy marriage. If this were true, then what about all those marriages where sexual intercourse is not possible due to health conditions, chronic sickness/illness, disabilities, age, physical ability, or trauma? God did not create sex to be a requirement for a healthy marriage. God's requirements for a healthy and God-honoring marriage are laid out in Ephesians 5:22-32. I do believe that every married couple should have sex at least once, preferably at the very beginning of their marriage to consummate their marriage vows and to fulfill the command of the "two shall become one flesh." Of course, there will always be exceptions to this rule (see above examples) as to why a married couple may not be able to have sexual intercourse.

One of the most common questions I receive is, "Is it sinful to get married but not want children?"

It is certainly not sinful to not physically conceive children. If it were, then there would be a lot of guilt-ridden wives out there who desire to conceive children but cannot for a myriad of reasons. However, I would encourage any married couple who does not desire to conceive children of their own to consider the purpose of multiplying in sex: evangelism and discipleship of our offspring. Aside from conceiving their own children, there are other ways to be intentional about expanding their family in ways that are glorifying to God, such as foster care and adoption. I would hope that couples who intentionally do not want to conceive children of their own for whatever reason would choose abstinence in their marriage so that they would not have an unwanted pregnancy.

If they choose to have sex, then I would recommend that they pray earnestly about being content and grateful if God were to bless them with a child and that they would see it as another opportunity for their faith to be strengthened and to serve the Lord faithfully.

For the married couple who does not want children at all added to their family, then I would apply the same opinion that the Apostle Paul gives in 1 Corinthians 7, that those who choose not to have any children should do it for pursuing an undistracted devotion to serving the Lord with their marriage.

What about 1 Corinthians 7:5, "Stop depriving one another, except by agreement for a time, so that you may devote yourselves to prayer, and come together again so that Satan will not tempt you because of your lack of self-control."?

This is the most common objection to my view on abstinence in marriage. I would argue that the culture of the first century was still a culture that generally still treasured childbearing positively and did not view it as some kind of obstacle in life that would get in their way of fulfilled living. Whereas the American culture has become increasingly resistant towards child-bearing, which can easily be seen in just the rates of abortion (the murder of unborn babies) and single-parent homes.

With that being said, I certainly do not support husbands

and wives to "deprive" each other as those who the Apostle Paul was writing to in 1 Corinthians, but I do believe there is a significant difference between a culture that is not opposed to children and a culture that generally views children as some sort of burden or obstacle. Once again, this is one of the ways that applying the principles of P.L.U.M. aim towards protecting the sanctity of sex. Married couples who want to enjoy sex without having the concern of having children, should consider that God created sex with four purposes to be enjoyed together, not just one or two of them. Simply put, those who want to enjoy sex but do not want children (regardless whether or not they already have children), P.L.U.M. would suggest that they abstain until they have a peace about the possibility of having a child (or another child).

Abortion and Unwanted Pregnancies

Abortion and unwanted pregnancies both share a similar feeling towards the child in utero: the child is an inconvenience. Multiplying in sex is to reflect God's desire to grow His kingdom. Abortion and unwanted pregnancies are the exact opposite of that. Just as there is rejoicing in the presence of the angels of God when one sinner repents (Luke 15:10), then the anticipation of another child coming into the world should be met with the same amount of excitement. Pregnancies should not be associated with feelings of disappointment or regret, because of the great value that God places on the life of every conceived child. Modern abortion can be compared to the nation of Israel being guilty of sacrificing their children to the false god Molech (Leviticus 20:1-5) in that not only is it considered murder, but it is also placing a lesser value on children than that of other human beings who have also been created in the same image of God.

Those who have had an abortion in the past can rest assured that if their faith is in Jesus Christ, God will redeem their past for His glory. Remember that no sinful act can thwart God's sovereignty in causing all things to work for the good of those who love Him (Romans 8:28).

Surrogacy

Although surrogacy can be done with the most loving and good-willed intentions, God's design for mothers is to raise the children that are born from their own bodies. Many studies show the unique physiological bond between a baby and its mother. Therefore, I believe moms who cannot bear children (or do not bear children in their desired timing) should either wait patiently on what God has for them or decide to adopt a child in need of a home.

Genesis 16 tells us a more tragic story of surrogacy where Abram and Sarai were promised a son. When it didn't happen in the time they expected it to, they turned to a surrogate for Abram to have sex with. They ended up having a son together (Ishmael, to whom Islam traces its origins). Abram and Sarai assumed Ishmael was the son God promised them, but as it turned out, God told them that the son He promised is going to come directly from Sarai's body (at 90 years old!). Sure enough, that son was born exactly when God said it would, and his name was Isaac.

Unfortunately, financial gain has also become a significant factor in surrogacy. There is a lot of money that can be made for a woman who is willing to use her body to carry and bear a child for another woman who may not able to do it for herself. This is another example of how bearing children can be used for selfish gain and not for the ultimate gain for the Kingdom of heaven.

Erectile Dysfunction

Similar to women who are not able to conceive, I would encourage men who struggle with erectile dysfunction to trust the Lord in their struggle by abstaining from medications in attempts to help them. This, of course, can get very complicated as to what qualifies as "medication." If it is something as simple as eating a healthier diet or exercising more that will help them, then I would certainly say those are good things to do.

My main concern in the matters of erectile dysfunction, IVF, artificial insemination, and the like is that as technology continues to advance, human beings will be more and more able to get what they want, when they want it, and how they want it. I believe that God would rather have His people practice patience and contentment, rather than seeking to achieve and obtain everything their heart desires. Jesus said that it would be a shame for a person to "gain the whole world, and yet forfeit their soul" (Matthew 16:26).

Patience and contentment are interesting concepts in that people will typically only be patient and content when they absolutely must. If they have the ability to get what they want when they want it, seldom would any person wait and be content.

For the man who struggles with erectile dysfunction, I would encourage him to seek to please the Lord in continuing growing to be the husband described in Ephesians 5. The husband will likely struggle with the societal pressures and norms of what it means to perform sexually as a man, and he will be comparing himself to the worldly views of manhood instead of the biblical view of manhood.

How does P.L.U.M. apply after menopause?

Many women have asked me, "How does the multiplying purpose of sex apply after menopause? Would I be sinning by having sex with my husband even though I cannot conceive anymore?"

Once again, we must remind ourselves of the purpose of multiplying in sex: evangelism and discipleship of our offspring. I have very good news for wives who are past their child-bearing years: continue to enjoy sex! Menopause should be considered a significant milestone to be reached, and you should celebrate.

It is God's natural design for men and woman to not be able to conceive children past a certain point in their lives, and that design can be celebrated. This is another reason why I think people should try to have children sooner rather than later because God designed us to generally be more energetic and physically able in our younger years, which is ideal for raising children.

Wives can simply enjoy sex after menopause because the chapter of conceiving more children has ended. If she is already a mother, then certainly her responsibility of evangelizing and discipling her children is not finished until she is taken home to be with the Lord. If the woman is not a mother, then she can still devote herself to evangelism and discipleship of others.

Sexual Abuse

Most of the time when I present the P.L.U.M. seminar, near the end I will bring up the topic of how P.L.U.M. applies to sexual abuse. I go into every seminar with the understanding of the reality that in a room of 50 people, it is likely that at least 10 of those people have probably been sexually abused at some point in their life. I am simply going to write here what I try to communicate verbally in my seminars to those who have been abused:

Deuteronomy 22:25-27 (NASB) states,

> *But if in the field the man finds the girl who is engaged, and the man forces her and lies with her, then only the man who lies with her shall die. But you shall do nothing to the girl; there is no sin in the girl worthy of death, for just as a man rises against his neighbor and murders him, so is this case. When he found her in the field, the engaged girl cried out, but there was no one to save her.*

Feelings of guilt

In many cases of sexual abuse, there tends to be a commonality in that those who were abused deal with feelings of guilt, that they are somehow responsible for what happened to them. They will struggle with thoughts like: "I could have done more to stop it" or "Maybe I deserved it," and similar thoughts. Christians worship a God who is omniscient (all-knowing), and we see explicitly in the Deuteronomy passage that the girl who was raped cried out, and even though there were no witnesses or anyone available to save her, God made it abundantly clear to the nation of Israel that they do nothing to the girl in terms of punishment, and only stone the man to death.

Those who cried for help (internally or externally)

I believe everyone who was abused cried out in some form. Whether they physically resisted, verbally cried for help, or in fear of being hurt even more, they chose to remain silent outwardly but were internally pleading for it to stop. The fact of the matter is this: something was done to them that was against their desire, and that is all that matters to God in the case of Deuteronomy 22:25-27.

Conclusion

If you have been abused, you need to know that God knows exactly what sin you are guilty of and what you are not guilty of. In the case of being sexually abused, and having something done to you that was against your desire, God does not find you guilty of any sin in that circumstance. God does not blame you for what happened, and neither should you.

In addition, pray for the soul of the one who abused you, that they genuinely repent of their sin so that their life might be redeemed from their sinful state. I know this is much easier said than done, but it is also a command directly from God (Matthew 5:44).

Remember to pray for your own healing, remembering that all things are redeemable in Christ Jesus (2 Corinthians 5:17). Regardless of our sin, wounds, and struggles, God's healing grace will abound all the more (Romans 5:20-21).

I pray these biblical truths are helpful to someone who has been abused.

13

How P.L.U.M. Preaches the Gospel

Husbands and wives, make your sex life an act of worship to God by understanding how even the purposes of sex can preach the Gospel.

When we understand that each purpose of sex reflects very specific aspects of God's image, we can have a better appreciation for what Christ accomplished on the cross for our behalf through His death and resurrection.

Pleasure:

The immense pleasure in sex should reflect the pleasure that God has in redeeming His people from their sin. Not only is this experienced through the orgasmic pleasure that can result from sex, but it can also be experienced simply through the pleasure that two people should have in offering their bodies to one another in the most vulnerable way possible. Jesus did this for us by being obedient to the point of death on the cross (Philippians 2), and God was actually "pleased to crush Him" so that many will be justified (Isaiah 53:10-11).

When Christians experience the awesomeness that is sex, the pleasure they receive from it should bring to mind the reason why God made sex pleasurable—to be a reflection of the fact that God was pleased to send His Son, Jesus Christ, to die for us sinners so that we could be redeemed for His glory.

Love:

The feelings of love that occur before, during, and after sex should reflect the same kind of love that God has for those He redeemed. This would also be the same kind of love that Christians are to have for their enemies, their neighbors, and themselves. The two greatest commandments that Jesus gave us sum up the entire law of Moses: Love God with all your heart, soul, mind, and strength, and love your neighbor as yourself.

When Christians have the kind of sex that reflects the love of God, they should be reminded of the various passages in the Bible that describe the kind of love God has for us: John 3:16, Romans 8:38-39, Ephesians 5:25-27, 1 John 4:10, and many others. God's love for His redeemed is complete, unconditional, immeasurable, committed, and sacrificial.

Unity:

The unifying purpose of sex should reflect the eternal and unbreakable relationship that every believer has with God through Jesus Christ. Christians are eternally bonded to Christ and are sealed by the Holy Spirit for the day of redemption (Ephesians 1:13-14). As those who have been redeemed and recipients of God's love through Jesus Christ, we have the joy of knowing that our relationship with God is everlasting, and that He will never leave us nor forsake us (Hebrews 13:5).

When Christians have sex that reflects the same kind of unity that God has with those He redeemed by the blood of Jesus Christ, they can have a better appreciation for the unbreakable bond they have with the God who loves them and was pleased to lift them out of the miry clay—their sinfulness.

Multiplying:

The multiplying in sex should reflect God's desire to continually grow His kingdom. Every Christian should be continually thankful for the fact that God sought them out in their sinful state, and while they were still enemies of God, Christ died for them so that they could be reconciled into peace with God instead of remaining in enmity with God. Christians are walking testimonies of God's desire to continually grow His kingdom, because their salvation was a result of God's desire for them.

This appreciation for being a part of God's plan of salvation should then be enough motivation for the Christian to want to preach the gospel to others and reflect God's desire to grow His kingdom in their thoughts and actions towards others.

When Christians have sex and it results in pregnancy, their #1 purpose for that child should be to teach them to love and fear the Lord and to know Jesus Christ so that they too might be saved. Even though parents do not have control over whether or not their child goes to heaven, they have the God-given responsibility to preach the gospel to them (Deuteronomy 6, Matthew 28:19-20, Ephesians 6:4) continually in a way that mirrors God's desire to see His kingdom grow in righteousness.

As a result of these findings, this is my conclusion: When the four purposes of sex are used properly, they work together to protect the sanctity of sex.

Imagine sex that includes all the following:

• Mutual pleasure (PLEASURE) in the giving of each other's bodies to one another that results in feeling completely vulnerable yet safe with one another,

• Unconditional love (LOVE) of God that ensures the partner that there is no hidden agenda or uncommunicated expectation of them,

• Feeling drawn closer to one another in a way that communicates the unbreakable bond (UNITY) the couple should have with one another and the security that they will not be separated in this life,

• Faith that is prepared to raise a child to know and love the Lord (MULTIPLYING) and that God will provide them with whatever they need to accomplish the task.

That is what sex should be like, each and every time a man and woman come together.

Conclusion

We can see that the beauty of the Gospel can be understood and more greatly appreciated through God's four purposes of sex. So Christians, next time you have sex with your husband or wife, take a little time afterwards with your spouse to reflect upon the riches of Christ that have been bestowed upon you, so that even your sex life can be an act of worship to the God that is pleased by you, loves you, is eternally bonded to you, and wants you to be a part of His growing kingdom.

Reflection Questions

• Have you ever considered how sex relates to the Gospel?

• How does thinking about sex in this way affect your commitment to sexual purity?

• What other topics/issues regarding sexual topics would you have liked to see discussed in this book? You can email them to wong.corwin@gmail.com

• How has this book helped you in your discernment on sex-related topics?